OPPORTUNITIES

in

Cartooning and Animation Careers

OPPORTUNITIES

in

Cartooning and Animation Careers

REVISED EDITION

TERENCE J. SACKS

New York   Chicago   San Francisco   Lisbon   London   Madrid   Mexico City
Milan   New Delhi   San Juan   Seoul   Singapore   Sydney   Toronto

The McGraw·Hill Companies

Library of Congress Cataloging-in-Publication Data

Sacks, Terence J.
  Opportunities in cartooning and animation careers / by Terence J. Sacks. — Rev. ed.
      p.   cm.
  Includes bibliographical references.
  ISBN 0-07-148206-7 (alk. paper)
    1. Animation (Cinematography)—Vocational guidance—United States.
  2. Cartooning—Vocational guidance—United States.   I. Title.   II. Title:
  Opportunities in cartooning and animation careers.

  NC1765.S23   2007
  741.5023'73—dc22   2007010426

1 2 3 4 5 6 7 8 9 10 11 12 13 14 15 16 17 18 19   DOC/DOC   0 9 8 7

ISBN 978-0-07-148206-6
MHID   0-07-148206-7

Interior design by Rattray Design

McGraw-Hill books are available at special quantity discounts to use as premiums and sales promotions, or for use in corporate training programs. For more information, please write to the Director of Special Sales, Professional Publishing, McGraw-Hill, Two Penn Plaza, New York, NY 10121-2298. Or contact your local bookstore.

This book is printed on acid-free paper.

Contents

Foreword ix

1. **Some Straight Talk About Cartooning and Animation** 1

What is a cartoon? The marketplace. Syndication is the ticket. Comic books enter the picture. Animation: a bright future. The Internet. Rocky road to success. Success can mean power, influence, and money. Cartoons are powerful in TV viewership. Profile: comic strip, comic book, and newsmagazine artist. Profile: senior instructor in animation.

2. **Cartooning and How It Developed** 23

European origins. Cartooning in America. Cartoons that move—animation. Profile: columnist and cartoon writer. Profile: senior animator.

3. An Overview of the Work 41

Cartooning for magazines. Panel cartoons or comic books. Calendars. Newspaper comic strips. Animated features. Profile: comic strip and comic book artist. Profile: professor and former Disney producer and animator.

4. What It Takes 67

Cartooning itch. Drawing and writing talent. Point of view. Character development. Getting over rough spots. Educational requirements. Profile: greeting card and comic strip cartoonist. Profile: director of animation in a college film department.

5. Getting Started 83

Newspapers versus magazines. Beating the rejection blues. Courting ideas. Many ways to skin a cat. An open field. How pay is figured. Earnings—what you can expect. Pros and cons of a cartooning career. What animation has to offer. Profile: cartoonist and illustrator.

6. A Glimpse at the Future 101

Newspaper cartoonists. Comic books. Magazines. Animation fast tracks. Two successful animation schools. Profile: video editor and animation teacher.

Appendix A: Major Newspaper Syndicates   109
Appendix B: Organizations   113
Appendix C: Periodicals   117
Appendix D: Schools   121
Further Reading   141

Foreword

Terry Sacks has done a fine job creating an overview of the cartooning field. His distinct categories of animation, panels, strips, editorial, and illustration cartoons offer an accurate description of the medium. His enthusiasm for the art form is present on every page, and his desire to educate and entertain will be genuinely felt by the reader.

Cartooning's future, whether in publishing, film, broadcast, or on the Internet, seems bright. Terry's book is a very good introduction to this appealing mode of expression.

Jim Rohn
Columbia College
Chicago, Illinois

1

SOME STRAIGHT TALK ABOUT CARTOONING AND ANIMATION

Now LET'S GET this straight right from the start. Cartooning and, to a lesser extent, animation are not for the weak-minded or those seeking a nice stable income. The fields are expanding to be sure, and there are big bucks to be made if you have what it takes: talent, drawing skills, ability to meet deadlines, and, above all else, persistence—loads and loads of persistence. Even if you have all of these attributes, you may not be able to make it, especially in cartooning. Why do we say this? Because to make big money in cartooning, you have to be syndicated; that is, one of the major syndicates (see Appendix A) must be willing to take you on. Unfortunately, your chances of becoming syndicated are very slim indeed. For example, one major syndicate, King Features Syndicate, says that of the five thousand or so cartoons, comic strips, and so forth it receives every year, only *three* are accepted. And even if your strip is accepted, the syndicate will probably pay you only several thousand dollars a year for it. If at the end of the year, the syndicate does not make enough money selling your strip to newspapers, magazines, comic books, and the like, it will drop you, and you will be right back to square one. So you can see why we say that your chances of making it in cartooning are almost nil.

Now, animation is a completely different story, as you will see later in this chapter and in Chapters 2 and 3. Simply put, animation is a technique by which filmmakers use cartoons to create the illusion of motion (*animation* means "to give motion" or "life"). Animation is a booming industry, and people are needed to fill all sorts of technical and creative slots.

Why is it so important to be syndicated? The answer is simple. Syndicates have the power to distribute, promote, and sell your cartoon or comic strip to many hundreds of newspapers, magazines, comic book publishers, and so forth all over the United States and Canada. They handle dozens of cartoons and comic strips. It would be impossible for you to get the exposure on your own that syndicates can supply. But their requirements are very rigid, and it takes a minor miracle to meet them, even if you have the talent and creativity. We'll discuss more about syndication later on. For now, let's concentrate on the cartoon market, which, as we have said before, is expanding in many areas but has a very limited number of openings, even for the most talented of cartoonists.

What Is a Cartoon?

To put it simply, a cartoon is a series of drawings, usually humorous, that tells a story or imparts a message. Sometimes, though, cartoons or comic strips—the terms are often interchangeable—can be grim and thought provoking. Bill Luckavich, a political cartoonist for the *Atlanta Journal Constitution*, recently won the top award of the National Cartoonists Society by doing a cartoon in which he had the names of the then twenty-five hundred or so casualties of the war in Iraq spelled out to form the word "WHY" with a question mark. Bill Mauldin's cartoons of the American fighting forces in World War II told of the incredible hardships our soldiers had to face. (For a list of cartooning and animation organizations, see Appendix B.)

Usually, cartoonists tell their stories through a combination of words and drawings, but sometimes they let the drawings or cartoons speak for themselves. Another thing about cartoons, although drawings are based on real-life figures, cartoonists almost always exaggerate some feature of the subject, such as the head, nose, hands, or feet. This exaggeration is called *caricature*. For example, normally the human head takes up about an eighth of the length of the body, but in a cartoon, the heads of the characters may be a third of the body's total length. Or the nose or ears may be grossly exaggerated. This enables the cartoonist to concentrate on certain distinctive features and to insert a sneer or a leer (or a smile) on the character's face. For now, let's look at the five basic groups that comprise cartoons, as well as the special skills required and challenges posed by each: editorial or political cartoons; comic strips, panels, and comic books; gag or magazine cartoons; illustrative cartoons; and animated cartoons, which, like movies or films, can be projected onto a screen.

Editorial or Political Cartoons

With the editorial or political cartoon, the cartoonist tries to do with drawings what newspaper editorials do with words. A feature of newspapers and magazines, the editorial cartoon—usually a single drawing with or without captions—attempts to sway readers to adopt a certain opinion on some timely issue. Quite often such cartoons relate directly to a particular event in the news.

Often editorial cartoonists use a special symbol to help convey their meaning quickly and simply. For instance, one of the most famous American cartoonists, Thomas Nast, drew a ferocious tiger (representing Tammany Hall, the corrupt New York political machine) attacking a beautiful young girl (representing the innocent public lying helpless on the ground). Nast is also credited with introducing the elephant as the long-standing symbol of the Republican party and the donkey as the hallmark of the Democratic party.

The work of political cartoonists is so powerful that it rates a special category in the Pulitzer prize awards. In addition to the abovementioned Luckavich, recent winners include the late Herbert L. Block (who would sign his cartoons as *Herblock*), Bill Mauldin, and John Fischetti.

Certainly one of the foremost political cartoonists working today is Pat Oliphant, an Australian native who began his career at his hometown newspaper, *Adelaide*, before moving to the United States in 1964, where he started work as a political cartoonist for the *Denver Post*. His cartoons have been distributed by Universal Press Syndicate since 1990. His numerous awards include the Pulitzer prize, two Reuben Awards from the National Cartoonists Society, and the Thomas Nast Prize.

Comic Strips, Panels, and Comic Books

You might consider comic books as a separate category, but we have included them in this category because they are based on such well-known strips as *Superman, Batman,* or *Dick Tracy.* Most comic strips and panels appear regularly in newspapers and magazines, and the content and tone of these comics are as varied as their readers. Some, like *Dick Tracy,* originated by the late Chester Gould, are adventure strips that continue their adventures day by day. Others, like the late Johnny Hart's *B.C.* and the late Charles M. Schulz's *Peanuts,* differ every day and are written for quick laughs.

A large metropolitan paper may print a page or two of cartoons and comic strips every day. Usually they appear in the same place in the paper, but occasionally you will find a single panel cartoon in the classifieds and/or other sections.

Usually, cartoon strips that appear during the week are printed in black ink, but those that appear in Sunday papers are typically in color.

Cartoon strips often are printed in the form of magazines as comic books and may feature a single story, a collection of stories, or a story that continues through many comic books or even indefinitely. They may also feature adventure or fantasy stories, such as *The Chronicles of Narnia* or *The Incredibles* or humorous strips such as *Teacher's Pet* or *Chicken Little.* With hundreds of strips in existence, comic books remain one of the biggest and most lucrative markets for artists with cartooning skills. Frank Miller and Alex Ross revolutionized the comic book industry by converting the books from a medium aimed primarily at youngsters to one that attracts many adult readers. Miller began the change with his four-part comic book series *Batman: The Dark Knight Returns.* The hardcover version made the *New York Times* bestseller list and remains in print. Ross's dramatic paintings have made him one of the most sought-after comic book artists, with his work appearing in both Marvel and DC Comics, two of the leaders in the comic book field.

A special kind of comic book, which was popular in the 1930s and 1940s, was the Big Little Books. Published by Whitman Publishing of Racine, Wisconsin, the books featured a hard cardboard cover, were about four inches square, ran about 432 pages in length, and included some of the most popular cartoon strips, including *Dick Tracy, Popeye, Red Ryder, Smokey Stover,* and *Little Orphan Annie,* to name but a few. But by the end of the 1940s, the books, which had been selling in the millions, had largely run their course and were discontinued when Whitman became a part of the Western Publishing Company.

Gag or Magazine Cartoons

These cartoons appear primarily in general circulation magazines, such as the *New Yorker* or *Playboy,* and feature single-panel drawings with a one-line caption or no caption and are invariably funny. Newspapers often print several gag cartoons throughout the newspaper—on the funnies page and on pages that could use some livening up, such as pages that have nothing but classified ads.

Gag cartoons amuse readers by poking fun at a specific person or group or at people in general. Some great magazine cartoonists have entertained readers by satirizing human flaws. These include the late James Thurber, Helen Hokinson, and Charles Addams, whose morbid but funny cartoons ran in the *New Yorker* for years and inspired the highly popular TV series "The Addams Family."

Illustrative Cartoons

Illustrative cartoons, very much like comic books, help to explain or illuminate textbooks, general reading books, stories, or illustrative books. In this category falls the incomparable Dr. Seuss, whose illustrated books have sold in the hundreds of millions, and the *Peanuts* books, which likewise have sold in the millions.

Another famous cartoonist/illustrator is Laurent de Brunhoff, who has written and illustrated more than thirty Babar books, which have excited the imaginations of millions of youngsters in seventeen languages. Originated by Laurent de Brunhoff's father in 1931, the Babar books are unique and feature adventurous and fashionable elephants that walk upright, wear glasses and hats, drive cars, and exist alongside humans as if there were no barriers.

Other examples of highly successful book cartoonists are the Berenstains (of Berenstain Bears fame), whose numerous books continue to delight millions of readers, and the late Shel Silverstein, whose *The Missing Piece*, *A Light in the Attic*, *Where the Sidewalk Ends*, and others are classics.

Animated Cartoons

The final category of cartooning is animation, a technique in which filmmakers use cartoons to create the illusion of motion. Here the filmmaker photographs a series of drawings one frame at a time. The position of the drawings varies minutely frame to frame, but when the frames are run through a projector, the subjects appear to move. Animation employing computers was used successfully by George Lucas, creator of the highly successful *Star Wars* films, and others to bring life to dozens of fantastic creatures that move, act, and speak as if they were three-dimensional characters.

Outside of the film industry, animation is found in a number of diverse fields. For one, it is often used by advertisers to highlight and sell their products, as in the case of the duck commercials produced for AFLAC Insurance. Animation is also featured in video and computer games like *Super Mario* and *World of Warcraft*, which are produced by companies like Nintendo and Sega. In fact, video and computer games are one of the most rapidly growing segments of the cartoon industry. Instructional film producers also often rely on animation to explain a technique or concept that may not be readily understood through live action.

The Marketplace

As a cartoonist, you have all of the above options to choose from in deciding how to apply your talents in building a unique and satisfying career. Just look around. You will find many other fertile fields to explore in addition to cartoon strips, such as illustrating greeting cards, calendars, shirts, and other items.

Unfortunately, one of the fields of employment for gag and political cartoonists—the newspaper industry—has shrunk considerably from a high of twenty-two hundred newspapers published in 1910 to about eighteen hundred published today. As you can imagine, the number of openings has likewise declined and the competition is fiercer than ever. But don't despair; newspapers and syndicates are still looking for that cartoon strip or panel that is a little different, such as Gary Larson's *The Far Side* or Mort Walker's *Beetle Bailey*. Another excellent example is *Watch Your Head*, an interracial strip by Cory Thomas that debuted in March 2006. With distribution handled by the *Washington Post* Writers Group, a national syndicate, the future looks bright for *Watch Your Head*.

Need further proof? How about Al Capp's *Li'l Abner*? His cartoon strip began in 1934 and was carried at first by only eight newspapers, climbing to several hundred more in three short years.

Before long it appeared in hundreds more, with a circulation of more than sixty million readers.

Besides entertaining millions of readers, Capp permanently influenced popular culture. His Sadie Hawkins Day inspired real-life girls to ask boys to dances across the United States and Canada. His lovable Shmoos characters became one of the largest merchandising successes in its time.

Syndication Is the Ticket

We have spoken before about the power of syndication. There are several major syndicates that will attempt to sell a cartoonist's creations to any number of newspapers and magazines. You get a certain amount of money for each paper the syndicate sells your strip to (depending on the circulation of the newspaper). This can often add up to quite a hefty sum. In recent years, however, syndication has taken a back seat to animation and comic books, the fastest-growing segments of the industry.

Comic Books Enter the Picture

Comic books grew out of cartoon strips and were first sold during the early 1930s, when such revered strips as *Mickey Mouse, Flash Gordon,* and *Dick Tracy* all made their debuts in books.

The year 1937 saw the start of such one-theme comics as Detective Comics, later to become DC Comics and the springboard for the extremely popular character of Batman, which was followed by the debut of perhaps the greatest of all comic book heroes ever—Superman.

Superheroes continued to dominate the field in the 1940s through such creations as *The Spirit, Captain Marvel, The Flash, The Human Torch*, and many others, reaching perhaps their height of popularity during World War II with *Captain America* leading the pack.

The postwar years saw the introduction of horror comics, such as *The Crypt of Terror* and *Weird Fantasy*. However, the mid-1950s saw the revival of earlier superheroes, such as the aforementioned *Superman, Captain America*, and *The Human Torch*. By the end of the 1960s, comic books looked a lot like they do today: an abundance of heroes, each with his or her own book.

The 1980s witnessed the rise of the graphic novel, which placed such heroes as Alan Moore's *The Watchmen* and Frank Miller's Batman in *The Dark Knight Returns* in more modern settings.

Today, Marvel and DC's domination of the industry has been broken by the debut of alternative comic book publishers, such as Dark Horse and Image, which run just behind Marvel and DC comics in popularity.

Animation: A Bright Future

Although overall the opportunities in cartooning look challenging, the future of animation looks especially bright for those who have the required skills. This rapidly rising field is going through a revolution fueled in part by high-tech wizards armed with graphics software and high-powered workstations.

Animated films, once populated solely by fetching beauties and ferocious beasts all drawn lovingly by hand, entered a new era with the release of *Toy Story*, the first computer-driven animated feature film and the first such film to approach the $200 million box office mark set by Disney's 1994 epic *The Lion King*. *Toy Story* grossed $358 million worldwide and $191 million in the United States. *Finding Nemo*, an Academy award–winning computer-animated film from Pixar, ultimately grossed $850 million worldwide.

In recent years Pixar released *The Incredibles* and *Toy Story 2*, and DreamWorks produced *Shrek*, all wildly popular. Released in 2006 were such hit films as *Cars*, *Barnyard*, *Monster House*, and *Happy Feet*, which beat the James Bond film *Casino Royale* at the opening weekend box office.

Even though in feature film, traditional cel-generated animation seems to be on the decline, most animated films are still produced by a combination of cel animation and computer graphics imaging. Disney's *Lilo and Stitch*, *Chicken Little*, *Tarzan*, and *Fantasia 2000* were based on traditional animation but also featured large doses of computer-created elements.

In DreamWorks's *Prince of Egypt*, more than half of the shots contained computer-driven effects. For instance, the seven-minute scene of the parting of the Red Sea required the work of ten digital artists, a two-dimensional artist, sixteen traditional animators, and two programmers. In addition, it took approximately 318,000 computer-rendering hours to produce the 600,000 digitally generated human refugees shown in the scene. Just think how long it would have taken traditional cel animators to painstakingly produce those seven minutes of film.

And that's just the beginning. With Fox TVs tremendous success in "The Simpsons" and Comedy Central's wildly popular "South Park," networks continue to search for the next great animated program.

The Internet

The shrinking of the newspaper and magazine markets for cartoon strips and comic books has created a vacuum into which the World Wide Web has plunged. And here cartoonists' opinions of the medium waver all over the place. Some like Lynn Johnston, the creator of *For Better or For Worse*, say of the Internet: "This way an artist could fill up a whole screen and not be confined to so many panels."

"Further," she adds, "there could be color and art just as there was when a comic strip took up a whole page on Sunday."

Finally, Johnston likes how the Internet allows her to keep in contact with her readers. Visitors can use her site to e-mail her or to catch up on installments of her comic strip.

But Robb Armstrong, creator of the syndicated comic strip *Jump Start*, has a different take on the Internet: "The Internet is just a wild bronco. Maybe if it was tamed a bit and taught to jump over little fences, it might replace newspapers. Right now, it's too wild. There's no editing, no control of somebody's fantasies out of their basement."

Others, like Jim Davis, creator of *Garfield*, caution against the Internet, saying, "The whole timing of a newspaper comic strip cannot be saved when you do music and stop-animation." He compares comics on the Internet to "reading out loud to someone only to find that it doesn't sound funny any more because it is spoken."

Rocky Road to Success

Cartooning can be a very lucrative business for the vast majority of comic strip artists—if they are syndicated. But, as we have seen, that's a pretty big "if." True, syndicated cartoonists can earn hundreds of thousands of dollars, depending on the number and size of the papers in the United States and Canada in which they appear. Although surveys can track the popularity of cartoons and comic strips such as *Calvin and Hobbes*, they cannot tell you that nearly every successful cartoonist struggles for years before he or she hits the jackpot.

Take *Family Circus's* Bill Keane, whose words of advice to would-be cartoonists appears later in Chapter 4. He had a solid foundation of freelancing behind him before he achieved success. He was thirty-eight years old and had worked as a staff artist for fifteen years for the *Philadelphia Bulletin*. He had also done freelance cartoons for major magazines at the same time.

Or take *Tumbleweeds* creator Tom Ryan, who had held numerous jobs to support his growing family. Eventually he landed a job at the bottom of the commercial art ladder. It wasn't much, but it was a living, and through it he learned the fundamentals of cartooning. Through his commercial art experience, he tried out several art and cartooning styles, eventually settling on the particular style that he used to create *Tumbleweeds*, now one of the most popular cartoon strips of all time.

Bud Grace, creator of the syndicated *Ernie* cartoon strip, did not start out as a cartoonist. He intended to be a doctor and was thirty-eight years old before he even began drawing cartoons. It took him eight more years to sell his first gag cartoon to the *Saturday Review*. As time went on, he sold more and more gag cartoons to magazines. Eventually, he submitted sample strips of *Ernie* to King Features and bingo!—they bought it.

Similar stories of adversity and struggle can be told about almost every successful cartoonist today. So unless you are truly certain that you want to work as a cartoonist, and you accept the fact that *if* you hit the big time, it might take many long years before it happens, you had best think about cartooning more as a hobby.

Success Can Mean Power, Influence, and Money

Although we have mentioned how tough it is to make it in cartooning, there is no denying that the few who succeed can not only make a ton of money, but they can also sway public thought in ways that others only dream about.

Take Al Capp, the creator of *Li'l Abner*. Capp's admirers ranged from actor-director Charlie Chaplin to writer John Updike to economist John Paul Galbraith. Author John Steinbeck called Capp, "the most gifted writer in the world."

Besides all of this acclaim, Capp's fame spread to the mass media. He was a frequent and outspoken guest on "The Tonight Show," spanning the reigns of hosts Jack Paar, Steve Allen, and Johnnie Carson. He also wrote his own newspaper column and radio show.

Charles Schulz, the creator of the immensely popular *Peanuts* cartoon strip, had his first drawings published in *Ripley's Believe It or Not* and then in a Catholic comic book series called *Topics*. His first regularly published cartoon strip, *Li'l Folks*, ran from 1947 to 1949 in the *St. Paul Pioneer Press*. But *L'il Folks* was dropped in 1949. The following year, Schulz approached the United Features Syndicate with his best strips from *L'il Folks,* and *Peanuts* made its first appearance. You can guess the rest of the story: *Peanuts* became one of most popular comic strips of all time. In fact, *Peanuts* ran uninterrupted for nearly fifty years and appeared in a record twenty-six hundred newspapers in seventy-five countries. Following his death in 2000, *Forbes* magazine rated Schulz "the highest paid deceased person" in America. In fact, it has been estimated that Schulz's income during his lifetime totaled more than $1.1 billion, and his estate has continued to garner many millions of dollars since his passing. In fact, reruns of *Peanuts* are still appearing regularly in newspapers.

Another artist to hit it big in cartooning is the abovementioned Mort Walker, creator of *Beetle Bailey,* which is distributed by King Features to more than eighteen hundred newspapers in more than fifty countries with a combined readership of more than two hundred million per day. But it wasn't always that way.

Following service during World War II as an intelligence and investigating officer, Walker was discharged as a first lieutenant in 1947. The following year, he completed the requirements to graduate from the University of Missouri.

He went to New York City to pursue his cartooning career. To survive he worked as editor of three magazines for Dell Publishing. His first two hundred cartoons were rejected, but he persisted. In two years editors started to recognize his talent, and he became a top-selling magazine cartoonist. He was on his way, and he has never stopped in his efforts to reach the very pinnacle of success as a cartoon artist.

Still another who has struck it big in cartooning is Gary Trudeau, whose comic strip *Doonesbury* was syndicated in the newly formed Universal Press Syndicate in 1970. Today *Doonesbury* is syndicated to almost fourteen hundred newspapers worldwide and is accessible online through *Slate.* In 1975, he was the first comic strip creator to win the Pulitzer Prize for Editorial Cartooning. In 2004, Trudeau granted *Rolling Stone* magazine an interview in which he discussed his time at Yale University. In addition, he was the subject of an extensive article in the *Washington Post* in 2006. He also appeared on "Charlie Rose."

Cartoons Are Powerful in TV Viewership

Also indicative of the influence of cartooning on our way of life is the Cartoon Network begun by Ted Turner eleven years ago. Without warning, the Cartoon Network has shot up to the undreamt of position of fastest-growing network within the Turner Broadcasting sector, beating out its Turner siblings TNT and TBS in the cable network. Such powerhouse cartoons as "Bugs Bunny," "Tom and Jerry," and "The Powderpuff Girls" have helped Cartoon Network to register $650 million in income and $241 million in cash flow in 2005, enabling Cartoon Network to finish among the top-ten highest-rated basic-cable networks.

Despite the fact that all of this is true and that there are many more who are earning a lot of money in cartooning, your chances of making a regular income—let alone millions of dollars—are almost nil, and you had better realize it. If you still feel that cartooning is the field for you, go on to Chapter 2, which presents a history of the field from antiquity to current times.

Profile: Comic Strip, Comic Book, and Newsmagazine Artist

For as long as he can remember, Philip wanted to be a cartoonist. "I always had the itch to follow this career," he says. Both his grandparents worked on a paper in Kansas City, and he would often visit them there. He was always amazed to see what the artists who worked in the art department were turning out. He would also visit another fellow, now retired, who lived nearby, and this older fellow would create some pictures to amuse Philip. In grade school, Philip would draw heavily muscled strongmen engaged in sports, and he also did personal strips of himself and some of his friends.

Philip ended up in art school at the Art Institute of Chicago because he always liked to draw. He also took communications courses. Then his undergraduate program at the University of Texas helped him to better communicate his thoughts on the drawing board. "I want to become a better storyteller," he says, "and I am currently working on a story. I have about ninety pages completed already."

For a number of years now, Philip has been doing a weekly cartoon strip for a small paper in Chicago that is widely distributed in many areas of the city. To his knowledge it is the only full-color strip in what is known as the *alternative press*. The strip follows a continuing story line that is interrupted now and then with jokes to enliven the plot. He says that perhaps the foremost cartoonist in the alternative comics is Ben Katchor, who was picked up by the *Village Voice*. But as far as he knows, his is the only alternative strip in the world that appears in full color.

He estimates that he puts in thirty hours a week on the cartoon strip, and he does a lot of additional freelance work, primarily in the area of magazine illustration. His comic strip work is unlike any other medium, and it is something that he is thinking about constantly. He is paid anywhere from $300 to $1,200 for the same work, depending on who is paying. He receives $100 a week for the comic strip he does for the paper. But most of his income comes from the magazine illustration work, which pays a lot better than his comic strip work; but that, too, varies a lot from week to week.

"You can probably tell that I am primarily interested in visual comic strips and not in creating gag cartoons like those that appear in the *New Yorker* and other well-known magazines. I feel pretty lucky. For one, I am doing what I want to do, and nobody is censoring my work," he says. He adds that very few in cartooning are making anything like a fortune. Cartoonists are, for the most part, just getting by—except for those cartoonists who make daily comic strips for syndicates.

His advice is to draw as much as you can and do only what you really enjoy doing. In cartooning, you, like many others, may come to it expecting to arouse a certain emotional feeling in your readers—sympathy, laughter, fear—but you won't succeed all of the time, he says, no matter how hard you try. You may think that you can work for greeting card companies or draw animals or whatever, but again, he says, stick to those things that interest you most. "In cartooning," he says, "you should not base your work on what readers want to see. That is the wrong way to look at it. Your work must come first and must appeal to you. If your heart is really not in your work, it will become tiresome and very difficult."

Most of the assignments Philip receives are through word of mouth. He doesn't send out work on speculation for editors. But he has done illustrations for *Entertainment Weekly*, *National Lampoon*, *Spy*, and, more recently, for the *New Yorker* and the *Yale Review*.

Syndication pays very well, he notes, but it's hard to accomplish. Each syndicate probably promotes two strips a year out of the hundreds that it views. Because of space limitations and the extraordinary censorship and editorial restraints, Philip just can't see himself working for a syndicate.

One of the hardest parts of cartooning, he advises, is making your work seem authentic and avoiding situations in which your characters are not believable or are affectations of your mind. It's also hard to take when you get an idea that you are certain will work and realize halfway through that it won't work in any way. To his way of thinking, cartooning has to be completely creative and original—where your mind is creating the entire concept. In the class he teaches, he finds himself trying to teach drawing, composition, gestures, and other concepts important to creating cartoons. He says, "All of these elements are involved in visual patterning rhythms and are part of the elements and skills that I believe you need to be a successful artist."

Profile: Senior Instructor in Animation

Gabriel has been teaching full-time for three and a half years and for three years part-time before that. He teaches in a college film and video department, working primarily in animation and even more specifically in computer animation.

Gabriel started in animation back in the early 1980s and was trained by a Disney veteran who worked in New York at the time. There he did cartooning and illustration for about six or seven years. It wasn't until he got a computer animation and modeling job at a large video game company that he was able to finally get back into animation.

Originally, he had intended to go into cartooning, but he then received two opportunities in animation, the first while he was still in school. One of the classes offered was in animation, and he took it more out of a general interest than anything else. His main interest was illustration, but he was very taken with the class in animation and subsequently entered the field, where he has been active since 1993.

Gabriel worked for the video-game company from 1993 to 1995, not only as a computer modeler and game designer but also as a computer animator. He worked at another company from 1995 to 2002 in various areas of game design—concept art, game design, three-dimensional modeling and animation, motion capture, editing, and cinematics, in which a kind of finished film gets woven into the game as a reward for finishing the game successfully. Then he worked on minifilms that were put into games. "So," he says, "I was doing films at a game company." Then, four years ago, a full-time opening became available; he had been working at the college part-time, so he threw his hat in the ring and got the job.

He still does extra work in his spare time. Last year, for example, he codirected a corporate film in Chicago; he has collaborated with several directors doing preproduction for live-action, in which three-dimensional animation is used to block out a live-action film; and he is doing a series of illustrations for another director who is making a documentary.

Gabriel advises that the companies that hire in this field can afford to be picky. What they usually are looking for are technical skills that are immediately applicable, but at the same time they are looking for long-term talent and sensibility for projects that they may not even know about yet. Usually, they hire someone for a specific task, but the smarter companies also look for people who can fill their long-term needs.

"Jobs in the game fields and video games are pretty much scattered all over the country," he says. "My former company is one of the largest in the country. But you will find video games in production in Texas and Florida and in the Southeast as well as the West Coast. This is less true of feature film. That is primarily an East and West Coast phenomenon because that where most of the funding and distribution companies are located."

As for computers, he says, what they do in animation is to leverage what you can do as an individual artist. Animation involves filming twenty-four or thirty frames per second, and to have one person generate all of that art is virtually impossible. What computers allow, he says, is one of two things: they allow team projects to become more lush, or they make solo projects possible.

Basically, he notes, you use computers to do all of the iteration—all of the frames in between the most important key frames. So what the computers can do is take an idea that one person has and use technology to complete the work.

One of the nice things that technology does for the artist, Gabriel says, is that you don't really have to move to the company headquarters to make the films; you have to move somewhere where you can get the work out, either through festivals or with a larger movie studio.

"The biggest challenge for an artist is doing a balancing act between offering potential employers what they need right now and yet being able to work on the skills that won't make you obsolete two years from now," he advises. "Also there has to be a balance between art and technology. I joke in my classes that what you really are trying to do is to turn math into art. All computers really do is calculations. And so what you really have to do is to stay on top of the process so that the computer is creating what you want and not the other way around.

"I always tell my students that if you let the computer tell you what you create, your work won't look any different from anyone else's."

2

Cartooning and How It Developed

In a sense, you could say that cartooning is as old as the hills, or perhaps old as the caves would be more apt, because many archaeologists believe that cartooning goes back to the caricatures and primitive drawings found on ancient Egyptian walls and Greek vases. As originally defined, cartoons were preliminary drawings for serious paintings and architectural drawings. It was not until much later, in the mid-eighteenth century, that cartoons began to satirize subjects for the amusement of readers.

European Origins

An Englishman, William Hogarth (1697–1764), is credited with originating the cartoon as a satirical drawing poking fun at an individual, topic, or place. He had all that it takes to be a fine artist, but his repulsion at the predominantly low morals of members of polite society drove him to take a high moral stance that zeroed in on seamy and contemporary themes. Thus Hogarth abandoned the traditional standpoint of creating art for the sake of posterity in order to lash out at the art of the period. He attacked his contemporaries more and more through his satirical engravings. Starting in 1732, he produced several series of engravings—*The Rake's Progress, Marriage á la Mode, The Harlot's Progress*—that were fiercely realistic. Indeed, their very realism disqualified them from the upper strata of the arts, which were considered the arena of mythology, gentle scenes, and portraits. But Hogarth's realism struck a nerve with his viewers, and suddenly there was a new kind of art in which techniques and emotions were bent to comment on social and moral issues.

Hogarth inspired other early notables in cartooning, primarily Thomas Rowlandson and George Cruikshank. Rowlandson (1756–1827) was England's first great cartoonist. He started as a part-time caricaturist but because of heavy gambling debts soon turned to drawing full-time. Working primarily on copperplate etchings, Rowlandson's complex, somewhat rowdy sketches poked fun at all levels of society, but he reserved his sharpest barbs for the rich and powerful. Due to the development of the technology of journalism and the increase in newspaper distribution, he was able to reach a vastly greater audience than Hogarth. Rowlandson's work could be regarded as a forerunner of modern cartooning, since one series, *Tour of Dr. Syntax*, used the same method of storytelling or continuity used by some of the comic strips today.

George Cruikshank (1792–1878), also English, was born when Rowlandson was already thirty-six and already making a name for himself as a social commentator. Largely self-taught, Cruikshank was creative, irrepressible, and possessed of a sharp sense of man's inhumanity to man. His etchings primarily satirized the rich and the powerful—industrialists, landowners, and corrupt politicians. Although regarded by many to be a lesser artist than his predecessors, he was able to reach a still greater audience, as the number of newspapers and those who were literate continued to increase. The modern meaning of the word *cartoon* dates back to when Cruikshank was about fifty. To many, he was the link between classical satire and the modern cartoon.

The evils accompanying the industrialization of England, which included pollution, child labor abuses, and various abuses of the working classes, became an endless source of inspiration for Hogarth, Rowlandson, and Cruikshank, resulting in an almost unbroken stream of social satire that lasted over a period of almost two hundred years. Many artists in England and other European countries protested the moral decadence of the rich and the wretched conditions of the poorer classes. Nowhere was this done more vividly and with greater impact than in the work of the great Spanish artist Francisco Goya (1746–1828). His *Caprichios*, published in 1799, was a powerful indictment of the human condition, and his savage imagery played a prominent role in the development of the nineteenth-century European cartoon as an instrument of protest.

The cartoon as an instrument of humor can be traced back to the Frenchman Charles Philipon, who is considered the father of the modern humor magazine. His magazine, *La Charivari*, which he launched in 1832, soon became the pinnacle of humor magazines, and cartoonists of distinction clamored to be included in its pages. One cartoonist featured in its pages was Honoré Daumier (1808–1879), perhaps the greatest of French cartoonists, whose lithographs deftly satirized mid-nineteenth-century France. Largely because of the success of *La Charivari*, the British humor magazine *Punch* was begun in 1841 by Henry Mayhew, who modeled its pages after the social criticism of Philipon. Soon it carved out its own niche and included in its ranks such talented cartoonists as John Leech, who lampooned British politics, and Richard Doyle, who created the magazine's famous cover. Later, other talented artists, including John Tenniel, Charles Keene, and especially the model *Punch* cartoonist, George Du Maurier (1834–1896), were added to its ranks. Throughout the nineteenth century, *Punch* maintained its lofty position as the leading humor magazine in Great Britain despite the rise and fall of numerous other humor journals, such as *Vanity Fair*.

Cartooning in America

Prior to the Civil War, American cartooning was based largely on the English and European tradition of caricature and lampooning. In colonial America, within the restraints of the Alien and Sedition Acts, England and the Parliament were attacked by many cartoonists, including the renowned statesman Benjamin Franklin, who was famed primarily for his drawing of a bisected snake, each segment of which was labeled with the names of the various colonies and that carried the legend "Join or Die." Although the cartoon industry's growth was stimulated by the development of commercial lithography and the 1829 election of Andrew Jackson, who was often attacked by cartoonists, cartooning had little impact before the outbreak of the Civil War in 1861. That year's election of the tall, homespun, and bearded Abraham Lincoln inspired many of the most savage cartoons of the period.

Following the Civil War, none of the cartoonists of the period were more famous than Thomas Nast and Walt McDougall, whose most famous cartoon *Belshazzar's Feast* is believed to have tipped the 1884 presidential election to Grover Cleveland. The cartoon showed Cleveland's opponent, Senator James C. Blaine, eating at a table groaning with food while a poor worker and his wife approach the table begging for something to eat. At the same time an Englishman, Frank Leslie, published a series of comic magazines carrying the work of William Newman, formerly a leading artist of *Punch*.

Panel or gag cartoons came into prominence in America during the 1840s with the invention of lithography, a new technique that enhanced the transfer of illustrations directly from stones to paper. This was much simpler and less expensive than copperplates and engravings. Starting with the *Old American Comic Almanac* of 1841, dozens of comic almanacs featuring single-panel cartoons of satirical and often low, but not pornographic, nature were regularly published.

The 1870s saw the rise of the first generation of funny cartoonists, whose work appeared in such widely circulated magazines as *Puck* and *Judge*. Many of these artists appeared in Sunday comic pages in the 1890s, but all were primarily panel cartoonists. Included among them were A. B. Frost, E. W. Kemble, C. J. Taylor, Charles Dana Gibson, and Thomas S. Sullivant.

Twentieth Century

The start of the twentieth century marked the turn toward sharper tones among a new generation of cartoonists. Preeminent among these were Carl Anderson (famous for *Henry*), George Herriman (*Fritz the Cat*), and Robert F. Outcault, creator of *Hogan's Alley*, which originated in Joseph Pulitzer's *New York World*. This immensely popular strip featured the Yellow Kid and dealt with life in the tenement world of that period.

From 1900 to 1920, Pulitzer prize–winning cartoonist John T. McCutcheon, beloved for his drawings of Hoosier youngsters in the summertime, dominated. He covered both the Spanish-American War and the Boer War for the *Chicago Tribune* and won the Pulitzer prize in 1932 for his grim comments on the Depression. His classic cartoon *Injun Summer* appeared in the *Chicago Tribune* on September 30, 1930, and was reprinted for many years thereafter.

By the 1920s a new kind of disillusionment set in, as seen in cartoons featured in such magazines as the *New Yorker* and *Vanity Fair*, which used the cynical gag cartoon as one of its primary tools. Since its founding in 1925, the *New Yorker* has published an estimated sixty-eight thousand cartoons, gracing nearly all sections of the magazine and always on the magazine's front cover. Its list of contributors reads like a who's who in the panel cartooning world and includes John Held Jr.; Helen Hokinson, who satirized plump society women; Gluyas Williams; Peter Arno; Otto Soglow, creator of the Little King; and above all James Thurber, considered by many to be the greatest American humorist since Mark Twain. This impressive stable of cartoonists took potshots at civic pride, boosterism, social pretension, and smugness. Their efforts were continued by other great names in cartooning, including William Steig, Charles Addams, Sam Cobean, George Price, and Saul Steinberg.

But it was the *New Yorker's* overwhelming success with gag cartoons that spurred more widely circulated magazines—*Colliers*, the

Saturday Evening Post, *Woman's Day*, and many others—to jump on the bandwagon and begin to feature panel cartoons. By the 1950s there was scarcely a periodical in the land that did not carry some kind of panel cartoon. The *Saturday Evening Post*, for example, was said to run about thirty cartoons a week out of about four thousand submitted. And the daily newspapers, which received most of their cartoon strips from syndicates, began to scatter their single-panel cartoons throughout the paper to give readers some lighter moments while they browsed through the classified ad sections. Some panel cartoons, such as George Clark's *Neighbors* and William G. Clark's *Side Glances*, featured middle-class humor. Others, such as those of George Lichty and Reamer Kelly, poked fun at just about everything. Famous cartoonists of the period included J. R. Williams, creator of *Out Our Way*, which tells the story of a small middle-class town in America; Gluyas Williams, known primarily for his *New Yorker* panels that dissected the suburban middle classes; and Fontaine Fox, creator of *Toonerville Folks* and its off-the-track trolley, whose talents with perspective and off-kilter horizons, poles, people, and vehicles made him famous and beloved. Fox's cartoon strip, the third-oldest daily cartoon in the country, ran for more than forty years.

The 1950s and 1960s saw panel cartoons growing increasingly popular with such artists as Jules Feiffer, David Levine, and Edward Sorel lampooning national fads and trends, politicians, suburban life, sex, nudity, and other aspects of society. The most popular series at the time were those using humor to comment on domestic situations: Ted Key's *Hazel*, about a sarcastic and critical maid who to all intents is the head of the household she is supposed to serve, and the innocent *Family Circus*, which tells the story of an average American home based on cartoonist Bill Keane's own home life, are just two popular examples. Bill Hoest's *The Lockhorns* portrayed bickering, petty American married couples with lighthearted humor.

Inevitably, cartoonists began to specialize, and today many devote their work to a single interest, such as medicine, fashion, the financial world, or the courts. Sports cartoons, popular for many years, depicted real-life sporting events, but sports photography gradually took over their place in the papers. A few practitioners, such as Bill Gallo, of the *New York Daily News*, whose work hangs in the Baseball Hall of Fame in Cooperstown, New York, still produce these niche cartoons.

As society changes, so do the cartoons and comic strips created to reflect and comment on social themes and issues. Although vestiges of popular old-style cartoons still remain in the Sunday pages, another kind of cartoon—characterized by sarcasm and without illusion about the human race—has emerged, as represented by Gary Larson's *The Far Side*, Dan Piraro's *Bizzaro*, and the work of Gahan Wilson and Ed Gorey. Leading the new American cartoonists are Jim Borgman, Steve Benson, Tom Toles, Signe Wilkinson, and the *New Yorker*'s Roz Chast, one of a growing number of women cartoonists who have come into their own in recent years. To this list should be added *For Better or For Worse*'s Lynn Johnston and other Canadian cartoonists, including Duncan McPherson and Sean Martin.

Cartoons That Move—Animation

As far back as the seventeenth century, when the Chinese attempted to give motion via the shadow play, man has attempted to animate images. In the nineteenth century, the Frenchman Peter Mark Roget demonstrated the phenomenon known as "persistence of image," in which a given image remains fixed in a person's mind for a fraction of a second after the eye no longer sees it. Thus, if you take a series of images, each minutely different from the previous one, and view them in rapid succession, you get the impression of motion. This optical illusion is the basis of the animated cartoon, as well as the principal behind the motion picture.

Zoetropes and Rotoscopes

In the 1830s, W. G. Horner, a British watchmaker, devised what was probably the first practical demonstration of animation—the Zoetrope, which was a drum consisting of a series of hand-drawn images in succession. As the drum revolved, the images appeared to move. Emile Reynaud, a French inventor, went one step further with the praxinoscope, the first projector to show moving images. It was the invention of the film camera, however, that made animation feasible. In 1906 a newspaper cartoonist and filmmaker, J. S. Blackton, made the first humorous cartoon film, *Humorous Phases of Funny Faces*, which was based on one turn of the camera crank, one picture. In this way, the animated cartoon was permanently anchored to the movie camera. In 1911, cartoonist Windsor McCay worked with Blackton to produce an animated version of his popular newspaper cartoon *Little Nemo*. However, it was McCay's *Gertie the Dinosaur* that really established animation as an art form. Entranced viewers saw Gertie dancing on the screen, balancing a ball on her nose, and pulling up trees.

But early animators had to find ways of making the new cartoon art profitable. First they had to overcome the primary obstacle—

the enormous amount of work involved in producing only a few minutes of film animation. And a number of technical processes were devised to accomplish just this. J. R. Bray and Earl Hurd developed the process of drawing on celluloid, the so-called cel process. Raul Barre developed the peg system, which allowed for the correct positioning of the animated drawings in front of the camera through the use of pegs. Max Fleischer, who achieved fame as the talented producer of United Productions of America (UPA) cartoons in the 1920s, invented a device known as the *rotoscope*, which was used in tracing live action as animated footage. And the first animation studio was established by Bray and Barre in 1915. Its impressive list of cartoon stars were mostly borrowed from such newspaper comics as the *Katzenjammer Kids*, *Krazy Kat*, and *Mutt and Jeff*. A few popular characters, however, were developed by studio artists.

Perhaps the most popular character of the silent era was Felix the Cat, created by Pat Sullivan in 1917 and perfected by Otto Mesmer in the 1920s.

Disney Revolution

About this time the legendary Walt Disney entered the scene and rented a small studio in Hollywood with his brother Roy as his manager and chief financial backer. Disney called for Ub Iwerks and several other associates who had worked with him in a short-lived venture producing commercials in Kansas City in 1919. He then proceeded to produce a series of successful shorts. The first, *Alice in Cartoonland*, featured live action and animation. Next, in collaboration with several associates, he produced a series called *Oswald, the Lucky Rabbit*, which though well received was dropped when creditors threatened to take several characters away from Disney, a mistake he never repeated. Undaunted, Disney promptly thought up a new character, Mickey Mouse. His first two Mickey Mouse cartoons were silent, but the third, *Steamboat Willie*, had sound and was an instant hit in 1928. With *Steamboat Willie*, Disney's reputation was firmly established. (Interestingly enough, Walt Disney did all of the voices in the Mickey Mouse films, starting with *Steamboat Willie* in 1928 to *Fun and Fancy Free* in 1946.)

Not content to rest on his laurels, Disney soon produced another series, *Silly Symphonies*, to accompany the Mickey Mouse series. Starring a different cast of characters in each film, *Silly Symphonies* enabled Disney's animators to experiment with stories that relied less on gags and sly humor than on mood and emotion. Eventually *Silly Symphonies* became a training ground for all Disney artists as they prepared for the advent of full-length animated feature films that was to come.

In 1934 Disney informed his animators that he wanted to make an animated feature to be known as *Snow White and the Seven Dwarfs*. Although at first this met with some skepticism, eventually everyone became swept up by Disney's enthusiasm, and the work began. The film took three years to complete, but no one could have predicted what a spectacular hit it would become when it was released in 1937. It was the highest grossing film of all time until the release of *Gone with the Wind* in 1939. Other full-length animated features like *Pinocchio* and *Fantasia* in 1940, *Dumbo* in 1942, and *Lady and the Tramp* in 1955 further enhanced Disney's reputation as a master producer of animated films. Soon every other animation studio was imitating Disney, with the exception of Max Fleischer's, which wisely gave cartoon hits *Betty Boop* and *Popeye* human characteristics rather than animal features.

Disney's main competition during this period came from Warner Brothers Studios, founded by former Disney animators Hugh Harman, Rudolph Ising, and Isadore "Friz" Freleng. At first the studio attempted to imitate Disney's success with animals. But by the mid-1930s, Warner Brothers developed its own distinctive, fresh brand of humor, which is still funny today. Also, rather than compete with Disney in the field of full-length feature animation, it concentrated on the animated short. In 1930 Harman, Ising, and Freleng created their tremendously popular Looney Tunes series. When they left, the studio parlayed the talents of other outstanding animators—Chuck Jones, Tex Avery, and Bobe Cannon—into a string of immortal animated cartoon characters including Daffy Duck, Bugs Bunny, Porky Pig, the Road Runner, Wile E. Coyote, Tweety, Sylvester, and many more.

In 1940 MGM made its mark on the animation scene by launching the "Tom and Jerry" series. This wildly popular animated cartoon was the work of two young and talented studio animators, William Hanna and Joseph Barbera. Barbera wrote the stories, made the sketches, and came up with the gags while Hanna provided the direction. They went on to win five Pulitzer prizes with this hugely successful series.

Then, a few years later in 1944, Gene Kelly realized his lifelong dream of dancing with a cartoon character by teaming with Hanna and Barbera to produce the impressive *Anchors Aweigh*. After the close of MGM's animation studio in 1957, Hanna and Barbera followed with a series of popular animated features for television, including: "The Flintstones," "Huckleberry Hound," "Ruff and Ready," and "Quick Draw McGraw." In so doing, Hanna and Barbera rescued the floundering animation field by offering more jobs for artists, writers, and technicians than any other studio since Disney in the 1930s.

Following a dormant period in World War II, the new UPA captured audiences with the fresh and slightly off-kilter characters Mr. Magoo and Gerald McBoing Boing. But a slump in the industry eventually led to the closing of several studios. Thus the successes of Ralph Bakshi were all the more spectacular. One of his greatest animated films was *Lord of the Rings* (1978).

Following a prolonged industry slump in the 1970s, animation rebounded, and none with greater success than the Disney Company, which launched an ambitious schedule of full-length cartoons based on its stock-in-trade, the musical fairy tale. Disney's efforts paid off with the continued success of such full-length cartoons as *The Little Mermaid* (1989), *Beauty and the Beast* (1991), *The Lion King* (1994), *Toy Story* (1995), *Toy Story 2* (1999), *Monsters, Inc.* (2001), *Finding Nemo* (2003), *The Incredibles* (2004), *Cars* (2006), and *Ratatouille* (2007).

On television, most animated shows are aimed at children and elicit little attention from grownups and critics with one very prominent exception—"The Simpsons." This phenomenally popular series, slanted toward adults, is based on adult themes and situations. Several other prime-time situation cartoon series include "King of the Hill," "Beavis and Butthead," "Family Guy," and "South Park"—which are still being shown successfully as reruns. Many other new shows are in the works by major television networks that hope to build on the success of these animation situation comedies. These include "Bratz," and "Atomic Betty."

Profile: Columnist and Cartoon Writer

Anne Marie is a veteran journalist who also writes a cartoon strip. She got her first job as a beat reporter for a small newspaper. Then in 1985 she landed a job on the staff of a larger daily, where she also had the opportunity to begin writing her own column.

At the same time, she was given the chance to write the continuity for a comic strip. "This seemed to offer a real challenge in that it involved a new world for me," she says. "Although, just like the heroine of the strip, I am a reporter who happens to have a column in a big city paper."

For the past ten years she has been working with an artist doing the cartoon, and before that, she worked for five years with another artist.

"The work is creative in that you have to think visually," she advises. "This is something you can't learn. There is no room for explanation. The pictures have to speak for themselves. This is not a moving picture. You have to think how the dialogue can move the plot."

The money is almost nil, she notes. Rather, she does it for the challenge of doing a script that will help move the comic strip along. It involves the ability to tell a story in a different manner. "In a way," she says, "it's like you are a little child making up stories, so you have to get to the point very quickly."

Profile: Senior Animator

Pasquale works for an animation studio in Portland, Oregon, where he is a senior animator hired to work in the computer department doing computer as well as other kinds of animation. The studio's main business is production of short television commercials. It also does commercials for some foreign countries, including England, France, and Germany.

Now a senior animator, Pasquale has been with the studio since 1996. When he finished school at Columbia College in Chicago, he worked at various production studios in the city. Through a friend, the studio saw his reel, which had many of the commercials that he had worked on in Chicago. He was hired, Pasquale says, because the studio thought that he could be trained to use Lightwave, a computer program the studio was using. They were willing to give him some time to become accustomed to working on computers. It was about a year before he felt that he had become familiar enough to use a computer to do animation. "As a beginner," he says, "I used whatever animation skills I had or could learn to do computer animation. I started animating a couple of shots, and slowly I got a little better and a little faster. After about a year or two, I felt more like I knew what I was doing and was comfortable doing it."

In most of the spots that his studio did, for example, animators first built a character in the computer and then manipulated that character on the computer. On another project Pasquale worked on for *Glade*, he took drawings, made them look like a kid drew them, and then interjected them into a live-action screen. He notes that they use the computer as a big camera and a compositing device, which saves them having to figure out all of the camera and animation moves.

Pasquale contends that any place with up-to-date equipment that you will need is a pretty good bet for a job. It's possible to do computer animation anywhere in the country if the right equipment is available. On the West Coast, for example, there are many studios. They've got a little more pull perhaps, he says, because most of the advertisers in Chicago and New York are used to going there to make a project happen. They know the studios and their abilities.

If you do have the right tools, he advises, you can always try for a job with one of the bigger studios, such as Disney, Universal, or Pixar. They have hundreds of talented animators at their disposal, so they can pick and choose whom they hire. "You can try to get in there, but it's hard," he notes. "If your portfolio does not show the talents they are looking for, they will tell you that. They do hire beginners. But unfortunately, most of their new hires are from Cal Arts (California Institute of the Arts). A Cal Arts résumé is like the Cadillac of the animation business. Disney and some of the larger animation studios recruit a lot of people out of Cal Arts because it trains all students in Disney's style of animation. Also, Disney has invested money in that school and looks there first."

According to him, job security is pretty good. Many of the studios hire people on a project-by-project basis. He notes that you could work on a feature for two years and when the feature is completed, they may fire you. Then you have to start out again and look for more work. He says that he would rather work for two years on something that people know about than on something that will never be seen.

Hours can be very hectic in this business, he cautions. For example, he knows people in L.A. who work fourteen-hour days and sometimes weekends. He notes that many studios in L.A. and other places on the West Coast are unionized. This guarantees that you will work for a definite period of time and that you will be paid at a reasonable rate.

Pasquale's advice to all beginning cartoonists is to start assembling a portfolio or reel of your best work. "Whatever you do," he cautions, "don't send the original. Send a copy, which is all they will require to judge your qualifications."

3

An Overview of the Work

As WE HAVE already seen, there are many routes you can follow in achieving success in cartooning. To name but a few, cartoons can be the basis for simple panel or gag drawings, strips for newspapers, editorial or political commentaries, comic books and novels, or as illustrations for children's books—*Cat in the Hat, Babar the Elephant*, the *Berenstain Bears*, and many others. Cartoons are also used as illustrations for greeting cards and as artwork for advertising spots. Cartooning is the lifeblood of what is perhaps the fastest-growing part of the industry—animation. Once you have polished your cartooning skills, you have all of these varied and exciting fields to explore in finding a career that's right for you.

Cartooning for Magazines

Many cartoonists agree that magazines are perhaps the best market for beginners. Although established artists predominate as they do in other areas of cartooning, your chances of having your work viewed and ultimately accepted by the art director or whoever is in charge of purchasing cartoons are better in this field.

For one thing, magazine or gag cartoons can stand completely on their own. You are not locked into any one character or stock of characters, as you would be in a cartoon strip or comic book, so you have a whole world of characters and topics to explore. Then, too, magazine cartooning can also serve as a springboard to other fields in the industry—comic books, comic strips, children's books, greeting cards, and calendars, to name a few, as well as working with other media.

Magazines are also a good market for you as a beginning cartoonist because many magazines publish quite a few cartoons each month and will pay up to $500 for a single cartoon. And many cartoonists find magazines more receptive to the work of beginners than newspapers and other forms of media. General interest or large consumer magazines are the toughest market for beginners to break into, but they tend to pay more for the cartoons they commission. However, they will look at your work, and if your cartoon is fresh and distinctive, you have as good a chance as anyone of seeing your efforts published.

In addition to the large, well-established consumer magazines, such as the *New Yorker* or *Ladies Home Journal,* there are several special-interest magazines that buy cartoons each month and pay almost as well as the consumer magazines. These include medical journals, the whole gamut of trade magazines (for the construction, health, retail, fashion, and real estate fields, among others), as well as men's magazines, religious magazines, sports magazines, magazines for children, pet magazines, and many others. Editors of these magazines know that their readers like to laugh as much as any other magazine readers, and they are always on the lookout for the work of skilled cartoonists.

Online magazines are also becoming, in ever greater numbers, a good market for all types of cartoons. In keeping with the times, online magazines are often the first place that readers go to look for their favorite cartoons.

Creating and Submitting Cartoons to Magazines

For magazine cartooning, as is true of all branches of the field, you've got to have drawing and writing talent as well as creativity, flexibility, adaptability, a deep and sustaining love of cartooning, and perhaps the most important skill of all, persistence. You've got to learn to deal with rejection, which almost all cartoonists face, especially at the beginning of their careers.

With that in mind, here are a few ideas for producing and selling cartoons in all of the cartooning fields:

• **Jot down some ideas.** Write down as many ideas as you can; then assess them and focus on the strongest.

• **Be sure your cartoons are in the right format.** For instance, do not submit cartoon strips to a magazine that uses primarily single-panel cartoons. And make sure that the cartoon is appropriate to the magazine field. In other words, do not submit a cartoon involving sports to a food magazine.

• **Pencil in your cartoon on heavyweight typing paper.** Don't start inking until you feel that you have the cartoon just right. Go over your pencil sketch with black India ink or a felt-tip marker. Be sure the lines are bold enough to reproduce well, even if the cartoon is printed very small.

- **Learn to work quickly.** You can hardly expect to make a decent salary if it takes you a week to draw a cartoon. Since the rejection rate on cartoons is so high, at least at the start of your career, you need to produce as many as fifteen cartoons a day just to sell a few a week.

- **When your ink dries, be sure to erase pencil lines completely with an art gum eraser.** Alternatively, you can use non-photo blue pencil (available in art supply stores), which will not show up in most reproduction work, thus avoiding the necessity of erasing pencil lines.

- **If you want to create a dry wash that will add shading to your cartoons, you can use diluted black ink or watercolor.** You can gain the same effect by using the side of a black pencil on the drawing, blending it with the tissue, then spraying it with a fixing agent to prevent smudging. Since many magazines use color in their cartoons, you can color your work with concentrated watercolor dyes, either applied directly from a bottle or diluted with water to tone them down a bit. Whatever your choice, watercolor paint or dye, make sure your black outlines are inked with waterproof India ink, because watercolors and many paint dyes tend to smear and can cause lines to blur or fade. You may prefer to color your cartoons with markers. These can be applied with India ink lines or with felt-tip pen lines without causing your ink to smear. After your ink dries, you can draw patterns on a color with colored pencils.

- **Neatly print or type the caption beneath the drawing.** Do not write in a word balloon, which is the style for a cartoon strip.

- **On the back of the cartoon, print your name, address, phone number, and e-mail address.** Put a unique code number on the back of each cartoon to help you keep track of the cartoons submitted.

• **Mail your cartoons in a flat nine-by-twelve-inch envelope.** Remember to include an eight-by-ten-inch piece of cardboard for protection. Hard copies are preferred, although photographic copies on disk are acceptable and can be sent to the person in charge of cartoons. Be sure to enclose a self-addressed stamped envelope for the return of rejected cartoons. Without a reply envelope, many editors will not even consider your work. Each packet of cartoons should include ten to twenty panels to give the editor a complete picture of the range and style of your work. If you send out a packet to one magazine each week, you should plan on creating between five hundred and a thousand cartoons a year.

Do you think you are up to challenge? It can take anywhere from a few weeks to even several months to hear from an editor, but once your cartoons are returned (this is, of course, assuming they are rejected), pack them up again and send them to the next editor on the list.

Although you could send several packets of cartoons to more than one magazine at a time, until you become more familiar with the market and the quirks of various publications, it is best to submit your work one at a time.

As far as compiling a mailing list of magazines that might be interested in using your cartoons, the hard way is to browse through the magazine racks at your supermarket or bookstore and copy the names of the editors, publishers, and so forth. A much better way is to subscribe to *Gag Recap*, a newsletter that lists in each issue the names, addresses, editors, and payment rates for dozens of cartoon-buying magazines. Or you could check out *Writer's Market*, an annual publication, and *Artist's & Graphic Designer's Market*. (See Appendix C.)

Tools of the Trade

Increasingly, computers are playing a big part in the handling of cartoon art. You should seriously consider having a personal computer—desk or laptop—in your studio. Not only can you use the computer to create your work, but many publishers prefer that you e-mail your work to them, or, if in color, send it on a CD. This saves them the trouble of scanning and preparing original artwork for publication.

A computer with a CD-ROM allows you to put an encyclopedia of thousands of drawings and many other reference materials at your fingertips. Also, full-color printers are increasingly affordable and can give you color effects impossible to achieve with watercolors or colored pencils. Many cartoonists use computers to print four-color samples of their work for portfolios and other applications. Many cartoonists also use computers to do their lettering for them, thus freeing them from hours of tedious pen work. Several software products on the market will enable you to create your own personal lettering style; then you can save it as a computer font in your hard drive. You simply print out your captions on a laser printer and paste them onto your original artwork.

What else will you need to create eye-catching cartoons? A fully stocked shelf of reference materials that contain many photos will help you sketch any object with greater detail and clarity. For instance, if you need to draw a knight with a lance knocking over a horse-mounted opponent, photos of these items will help keep your drawings accurate. True, as a cartoonist you do not need to draw realistically, but detailed drawings can help your readers grasp your cartoons more easily. You wouldn't, for example, want them to mistake a scooter for a motorcycle.

Panel Cartoons or Comic Books

Magazines are not the sole market for panel cartoons. There are also books featuring panel cartoons of many established magazines, such as the *New Yorker* or *Playboy* as well as the dozens of comic books referred to in Chapter 1. These comic books may feature adventure stories, such as *The Amazing Spider-Man* or *Superman*, or they may feature a collection of stories or a continuous story. If you're not one of the lucky artists who has his or her work featured in books published by well-known magazines or in regular comic books, it's up to you to contact publishers that specialize in producing these kinds of books.

To better your chances of having your book proposal accepted or even considered, you should send the publisher an attractive, well-crafted proposal. Your work should highlight some kind of unique character, such as a character from *Baby Blues*, the *Lockhorns*, or *Zits*, or one of the animals from Gary Larson's *The Far Side*, whatever you feel will interest readers. Submit your best cartoons—but not the originals, copies only. Include a cover letter explaining the theme of your book and why you believe readers will want it. Be sure to list any successes you have had as a cartoonist, including the names of any online or print magazines that have published your work. Again, don't forget to include a self-addressed, stamped envelope for the return of your proposal if it is rejected.

Calendars

Another good market for your work is calendars. Use the same procedure outlined above for submission of your work. Here you have to prove your ability to work in color through your sample cartoons.

Check *Artist's Market* and *Writer's Market*, both published by *Writer's Digest*. (See Appendix C.)

Newspaper Comic Strips

Millions of newspaper readers religiously pore over the comics sections of their favorite newspapers day in and day out, especially on Sunday. As noted previously, the number of papers being published has shrunk; and to make matters worse, they pay even less for strips today than they used to. Yet they remain a top market for cartoonists. So, what are your chances for having one of your cartoon strips accepted in this market? To be honest, not very good. Many cartoonists feel that before long every paper in the United States and Canada will publish exactly the same cartoon strips. Already, the same few popular strips are syndicated in papers all over the country, with few exceptions. However, there is always the possibility that your work will be accepted if it has something unique or new to say. Good examples are *Boondocks* or *Broom Hilda*, both of which speak to modern readers.

Submitting Your Strips to Newspapers

When submitting your work to newspapers for publication, the key is to create a unique cast of characters with fresh insights into today's society, such as Charles Schulz's ever-popular *Peanuts*. This strip features Linus, the somewhat simple and innocent little boy; Lucy, his bossy and sarcastic sister; the bumbling and not-quite-with-it Charlie Brown; and, above all, the superhuman dog, Snoopy. Or how about *Hagar the Horrible*, which features a fierce-looking Viking type of character who has a soft heart. Study the cartoon strips you enjoy reading and analyze just what it is that you like about them. Also, study their content and the themes, style of drawing, and characters. Then create several cartoon strips of your own. They should be concise and easy to grasp. Further, they should be true to yourself and to your life experiences—perhaps a teenager who is exploring various career options or someone who is having problems with the opposite sex or an office worker who is caught up in office politics.

Your sample comic strips should be two to three times the size of the actual newspaper strip. On heavyweight paper, lay out your borders, rule in your lettering guide, and pencil in your drawings. Make sure your characters' dialog runs smoothly from left to right. Follow the procedure outlined earlier in this section on magazine submissions. Ink your borders, characters, settings, and lettering, and when the ink dries, erase any pencil lines. It will take at least three weeks, possibly a lot longer, to create enough material— roughly eighteen completed strips—to submit to various syndicates. Incidentally, the King Features Syndicate publishes a detailed outline of the procedure to follow in submitting a cartoon strip for consideration. (See Appendix A, which lists the major newspaper syndicates.) Put your name and phone number on each strip, and don't forget the self-addressed, stamped return envelope.

Development Contracts

With luck—make that a lot of luck—the syndicate may send you what is known in the trade as a development contract, which pays around $2,000 to $4,000. This ties you to a given syndicate while it works with you to polish and perfect your work for syndication to newspapers all over the United States and Canada. At the end of the contract, the syndicate will decide if it wants to formalize your strip with a regular contract or reject the strip outright.

Although the precise contract terms will vary from one syndicate to another, basically they spell out what the syndicate will do to sell your work to as many newspapers as possible and that you will provide it with your best work and on time. Usually the proceeds are split fifty-fifty between you and the syndicate. Your total income will thus depend on the number of papers that buy your strip and the size of each paper. Normally you should have the contract reviewed by a lawyer, preferably one familiar with such documents. Contracts can be quite lengthy and full of legal clauses that are difficult for anyone, especially a beginner, to understand. But above all make sure that you retain the rights to the characters you have created so that you can license them to other markets, such as publishers of comic books or companies that make T-shirts, caps, balls, or any other items that could feature your cartoon characters.

Animated Features

Animation means the creation of movement. Before animation software and digital cameras came into their own, animators drew images or built models to photograph in many poses and postures. To create the illusion of motion, they photographed each object or image in sequence, developed the film, and ran the images together while filming.

To get an idea of what is involved, consider that to produce a full-length animated feature lasting about an hour and a half, you would have to have a million or more individual drawings, and the studio typically would need about a year and a half for drawing and an additional year or two for production.

This would be an impossible task were it not for computer animation. With computer animation, the process becomes easier, quicker—much quicker—and more flexible. Computer artists create images and save them in the computer memory. They take digital photos of models and save the images. They preview sequences, edit and adjust images, and create animated art without ever developing still photos. Being able to edit images on the computer enables the animator to refine them easily and repeatedly.

Through special effects the animator can introduce images or sounds into a motion picture or taped television production. The artists who worked on *Jurassic Park*, for example, developed their animated sequences by mixing computer art with digital photos of dinosaur models. They blended the images and the sounds. They inserted effects into the kitchen scene where the children, who were real actors, were filmed hiding in terror.

From Story Line to Storyboard

The story line is the basis for all films, live action or animated. Ideas for good stories can come from several sources. Quite often, story ideas originate with the animation crew. Experienced writers and story sketch artists are then assigned the overwhelming job of adapting a script for the cartoon feature.

The script is written and a *storyboard*—a kind of a huge comic strip—is built. Commercial animation studios have developed the storyboard into a unique art form. On the storyboard, the plot is laid out in a series of pencil sketches that are mounted and pinned up in sequence on bulletin boards. Dialogue and descriptions of the scenes appear below each drawing. A typical storyboard will contain dialogue and action not shown in the renderings. Through the storyboard, the central ideas and themes are presented visually in a detailed analysis of the film's development. It shows, for example, the characters' initial appearance and movement, detailed drawings of the backgrounds, renderings of scenes and sequences, and notes on music and sound effects. Through the storyboard, the animator tries to answer such questions as: Is the story clearly presented? Is it done effectively? What are some potential problems? By placing the basic plot on the board for everyone to see, it is hoped that ideas and energy will be released and that potential problems can be nipped in the bud.

Types of Animation

There are several kinds of animation; the leading varieties are discussed in the paragraphs that follow.

Paper Cutout Animation

In this kind of animation, paper figures are held flat against a glass pressure plate. The animator moves the cutout pieces against backgrounds mounted on the glass. A camera mounted overhead takes one, two, three, and sometimes four exposures between each movement. A superb example of this technique is *The Thieving Magpie*, based on Rossini's opera and made by an Italian animator. Such animation is probably best for plots featuring a lot of physical action. It doesn't work so well with stories that depend on detailed movements, figures, and facial expressions.

Puppet Animation

Animation of three-dimensional objects, such as puppets and geometric shapes, has long fascinated animators. Here the basic principles of single-frame movement and photography apply. The puppets used must be sturdy, freestanding, and have flexible body joints so that they will be able to be viewed from 360 degrees. In

is the equivalent of the live action film's set designer.
...ry scene and camera setup through drawings. Here
...he foundation for the animation by rendering back-
...ts for each scene, usually referring to the storyboard
... research materials. These layouts don't appear in the
...on but are crucial for positioning and perspective in
.... The goal is to provide a stage in which animators
...heir characters and effects, as well as a blueprint, to
...y the background painters. You must have superior
...y, mastery of human and animal anatomy, perspec-
...composition, and architectural rendering talent (that
...a pencil).

...Painter

...the layout artist's drawings and translate them into
...paint. Love of painting (particularly in gouache and
...is a must. In addition you should have skills in draw-
...lor and design sense, and the ability to adapt to vari-
...ainting.

...imator

...or, you must be able to express your ideas clearly,
...quickly with a pencil. Furthermore, you need an
...; of the skill of linear drawing. As a beginner in this
...d be skilled in the mechanics of drawing animals and
...on and be able to caricature not only features but
...ons, and situations. Your training should also include
...nimal anatomy, perspective composition, quick-

this kind of animation, the animator builds a whole new world of minisets suitable for the story, keeping in mind such elements of the process as scale, suitability, stability, camera access, and dramatic lighting.

Claymation

Many consider this animation technique, also known as *clay animation*, to most fully utilize the power of animation. Here, figures made out of clay are manipulated and moved in very small increments. The clay medium permits countless variations. One of the foremost proponents of this technique is Nick Park, a British animation artist who has won Oscars for his work. His short films include *Creature Comforts* and the popular Wallace and Grommit films—*The Wrong Trousers*, *A Grand Day Out*, and *A Close Shave*—as well as the full-length *Curse of the Were-Rabbit*. For a sequence, in which one of the main characters is munching a cracker, Park estimated it took him 288 exposures to create just twelve seconds of film.

Cel Animation

By far the most popular and perhaps the most traditional form of animation is cel animation. This process, developed by Disney, Ub Iwerks, Max Fleischer, and other renowned animators, utilizes layers of transparent sheets of celluloid. Through cel animation you can change a component—a single layer—within a scene without having to draw every element over again. It is easier to attain a finely sketched result if only one element needs to be redrawn when a change is required. When the cels and the backgrounds are created, they are placed on a mounted animation stand and photographed. Each cel has *exposure sheets*, also known as *bar sheets*, on which the crew records the sequence and order of various cel layers, the number of exposures given each layer, and the movements of the camera.

Careers in Animation Features

As is true of all feature films, in animation it is the director's job to coordinate the production from start to finish. It's his or her role to time the animation action and to blend all of the elements—story, animation, dialogue, recording, color, and music—that go into the finished product. The *animation writer* usually creates the story, defines the characters, and shapes the story line into its component scenes. Once the timing is figured out and the track is analyzed, these combined elements are polished by the *lead animator*.

At the same time, *background artists* produce the various backgrounds needed for the film. When the backgrounds are completed, character drawings are placed on top of them for photographing. At Disney studios, it may take as many as fifteen hundred backgrounds for a single feature.

Before production on the film can begin, *layout artists* must do extensive research and be able to visualize and illustrate settings and objects from many perspectives. They determine the way the character moves in relation to backgrounds and lighting and how the action will combine with other elements in the production. Since layout artists design and draw guidelines for other artists, including background artists, to use in their drawings, they need considerable know-how of what the camera can and cannot do, as well as excellent drawing skills in perspective and composition.

Live actors provide the voices for each of the cartoon characters before the actual animation begins. Their vocal performances give

the characters life. The recor
tor together with a graphic ch
ing is shown on an exposure
of each drawing, frame by fi
camera operators.

Usually various animator
scenes, unless the film is very
action points for the drawing
film. These are drawn on pa
tors—known as the *in-betwe*
to complete a given sequen
35-mm projector at a speed
the director and the animate
form each specific action or
a chair in a second, the direc
drawings, if each frame is to
ings may take two frames ea
ings needed. The animator
responsible for moving the
create a range of emotional
tor is much like an actor with
each character come to life,

The completed drawing
Checkers then make sure th
identified. Finally a *camera*
the cels. The *film editor* m
soundtrack. There are many
production areas that fall ur
of these specialized fields, y
layout and design.

Layout Artis

This position
You stage ev
you handle t
ground layou
and additiona
final product
the animatio
will animate
be rendered
drawing abili
tive, pictorial
is, talent with

Background

Here you tak
color through
acrylic paints
ing, strong co
ous styles of

Character A

As an anima
forcibly, and
understandin
job, you shou
figures in act
actions, emot
human and

sketch, and figure drawing. In addition, you should be able to solve problems in weight, balance, movement, space, and proportion. Cartooning ability is not an important consideration in this field.

Effects Animator

In this job, your ability to render natural and physical phenomena, such as rain, fire, and water, embellishes the drawn character action in each scene. You need all of the skills noted for character animators, and in addition you should have an inquisitive mind and a love of drawing the elements of nature.

Computer Animator

For this position, apart from your computer expertise, you must also have a strong background in drawing, painting, and design, as well as strong color sense and a firm mastery of classical animation techniques.

Two-Dimensional Animator

In an era when computers seem to have taken over in this business and three-dimensional animation has taken Hollywood by storm, two-dimensional animation may sound old-fashioned. However, two-dimensional animation continues to be an expanding and popular field, especially since classical two-dimensional skills are the foundation for most three-dimensional work. Two-dimensional animators develop their skills through life drawing, composition, and perspective courses—studying proportion, line of action, structure, and basic anatomy—while working in such areas as animation, character design, cleanup, doping, modeling, slugging, and storyboard rendering.

Three-Dimensional Animator

Three-dimensional animators should have many of the skills of their two-dimensional counterparts. Computers do not eliminate the need for skills in life drawing, concept drawing, composition, character design, and so forth. However, as a three-dimensional animator, you would deal more extensively with modeling, texturing, and lighting in a three-dimensional environment, often with the use of various software tools and packages.

Storyboard Artist

As a storyboard artist you would interpret scripts to create a storyboard. Usually this includes planning shots, visualizing the story before drawing it, and being careful to maintain the continuity of shots. Typically, you will start out as an assistant doing cleanup and revisions, eventually working up to preparing parts of the storyboard under supervision. The work involves a lot of cutting and pasting, drawing and quick-sketching, perspective and composition, and perhaps, most important of all, story development and interpretation.

In-Betweeners

Most animators start out as in-betweeners—the artists who help the animators and animator assistants complete the action of a scene. It may not sound like much, but is a very important step where you learn the basics of animation. An in-between is a transition drawing between two key drawings that distill the essence of an animated action. The in-betweeners fill in the action between these key drawings.

Computer's Role in Animation

Just how important is the computer in the creation of animation? Very important, says Randy Glasbergen, a successful cartoonist-animator. Says Randy, "The computer has become the tool of choice for creating color work. The computer gives cartoonists color effects that simply aren't possible with watercolors, markers, or any other media . . . Publishers, designers, and layout people often prefer to receive color cartoons on disk because this can save them the trouble of scanning and preparing original artwork for publication." Glasbergen's comments are equally valid for animators.

A major step forward was *Jurassic Park*, released in 2001, which used computers to create live, breathing dinosaurs. It was a challenge to create organic elements, such as hair and skin, with the computer. The film *Jumanji* took the digital creation of animals one step further. In this film, for the first time, we saw familiar present-day animals such as monkeys and tigers look and behave as they do in life.

Even with the enormous advances in computer technology, the task of creating lifelike human beings is extremely challenging.

Computers have also enabled TV commercial producers to merge existing footage of well-known actors such as Humphrey Bogart and Gene Kelly with newly shot animated footage. Such composites of real life and animated effects were also used successfully in *Forrest Gump* and in an anniversary episode of "Star Trek: Deep Space Nine."

How far can the computer go? Will it replace animators in animated films? Not very likely, according to Disney Studios, whose films have been using computer graphics to support animation features since the early 1980s. The computer is merely a tool, if an indispensable one, says Disney, in the layout of scenes and backgrounds and in the planning of complex camera moves and the production and painting of actual drawings in some scenes.

Computers can help produce magnificent effects that were once painstakingly drawn by hand, such as the clock scene in *The Great Mouse Detective* (1986) or the wonderful flying carpet in *Aladdin* (released in 1992). Computers are also routinely used to relieve animators of some repetitive tasks and are commonly used to operate both electronic and optical camera systems.

"The most important thing to understand is that the computer animation is not an art form in itself," says John Lasseter, the well-known animator-producer whose *Toy Story* was a watershed in the use of computer graphics. "The computer is merely another medium within this art form, such as pencils, clay, sand, and puppets . . . computer animation is not accomplished any more by computers than clay animation is created by clay." He goes on to explain that every movement in an animated scene must have a reason for being there. It takes an animator to apply the fundamental principles, such as timing, staging, flow through, and overlapping action. "I believe that *Toy Story* was the first computer-animated film to win an Academy Award because Tinny, the wind-up toy, managed to humorously and poignantly convey so many human emotions," he says. "All of the objects in the film have their own personalities . . . which serves to propel the film and to make it unforgettable." In short, says Lasseter, computer animation combines the techniques of graphic design, animation, story writing, live action, and computer science. But, as with any artistic medium, the most vital element that drives the work is creativity, which can only be supplied by the animator.

Importance of the Field

Commercial animation is as varied as the styles and techniques of animation itself. These days animators can find jobs working in feature films, television, the Internet, CD-ROM production, as well as product design/visualization, architecture, and interior design. Within these fields, animators can perform a variety of roles.

Profile: Comic Strip and Comic Book Artist

Denzel wanted to be a cartoonist since he was six years old. He remembers drawing posters for school plays and being known as "the kid who could draw" in his school in suburban South Bend, Indiana. He also frequently drew posters for the Cub Scouts.

After finishing school he traveled for about a year and a half, and when he returned, he set up a studio to do freelance cartooning. After finding out that the local paper published cartoons on local issues by local artists, he studied the paper to familiarize himself with some of the issues, drew a few cartoons, and brought them over to the paper. The paper bought several, and that was the start of a three-year relationship at the height of which he was doing four political cartoons a week.

Later, when he got to Chicago, Denzel did illustrations for the feature section of the *Tribune*, but his contact there decided to leave and the artist was left without any further assignments. "This is one of the hazards that you run into in this line of business," he cautions. "You meet someone who likes your work, and one day your services are no longer needed when the successor takes over."

Denzel has been freelancing since arriving in Chicago, with one exception—a two-year stint in which he put in about twenty-four hours a week on a biweekly publication. In addition, he was handling assignments in the art department for illustrations and political cartoons.

When the paper was computerized, he was laid off. He still does illustrations for it on a freelance basis, and these are fairly regular assignments. When he was working full-time, the paper paid him $70 per week for one or two illustrations. "It was nothing sensational," he says, "but it was steady work." He is still on the payroll, but it's all freelance work now.

What it amounts to, he says, is this: there are those who draw in a cartoon style, but all they are really doing is illustrating. The way he sees it, cartooning is both writing and drawing; if you do not write anything to go with your drawings, then you are an illustrator, not a cartoonist.

Denzel draws a lot of illustrations now, but he prefers to stick to cartooning, even though he started in political cartooning. His branch of comic book illustration doesn't pay very well, but it does offer a lot of creative freedom. If you can draw mainstream comics for comic book publishers, he says, you can do fairly well. So do those who do cartoon strips for newspapers, almost all of which are syndicated and appear in hundreds of newspapers across the country. These syndicates pay beginners about $20,000 a year to start, but, he notes, you can be dropped just like that if the strip does not attract enough readers.

Creating comic books is a whole different ball game, says Denzel. Those who work the big, well-known books, such as *Batman* and *Superman,* can make up to $60,000 a year. "But my stuff is not mainstream," he says. "You might have called it 'underground' twenty-five years ago, but today it is considered alternative. Alternative comic books are relatively unstable commodities. Right now, those who are doing them successfully can earn upward of the mid-fifties off their comic books alone. Frankly, while I would like to work mainstream and make more money, I like the freedom of expression that I now enjoy and can probably make more money in this area if I work at it."

The real money, he advises, is to be made by selling your concepts to the movies or to TV. He says that you can be talking about a sizable amount of money—$100,000 or more—but there are catches. They may, for instance, want the rights to the character you have conceived, which you may not want to give up since you can make a lot of money marketing the strip to secondary publications. So even though you can make lot of money, he says, you also can lose by giving up your character rights.

To him, the worst part of cartooning is the conflict between what he wants to do artistically and what will pay the most. As a result, Denzel has gone down some paths that, in the short run, have not paid so well. To be frank, he says, had he really wanted to do political cartooning, he would probably be in a more secure position than he is now. It's a good job, if you are lucky enough to get one, he says, and admits that he was with a fairly good-sized paper and had friends in the industry who were willing to help him. But he lost his job in political cartooning because of a change in the company authority. That wasn't what soured him on the business of creating political cartoons, however; he simply found it boring to do that type of work each day, and he didn't enjoy how conservative some of his coworkers were.

Denzel likes writing his own stories and working with characters that he has created, and he didn't have the freedom to do this with that particular paper. He finds that any work he does has to challenge him. He has refused work that he didn't believe he could handle. Once, when asked to do a realistic drawing of the president, he felt that this was not something that he could do well.

Ordinarily, though, he doesn't turn down work because he may not agree with a person's politics or philosophy.

"Cartooning is more than a discipline; it's a compulsion," he says. "It's something that you can't help and that becomes pretty much of an obsession." But, he admits, sometimes it becomes a grind, and then he hates the work. And he may find that his back starts to ache and his hands get stiff.

"You could say that in cartooning, the world is your oyster," he says. "Everything becomes fodder for your work. You may not be so hot in drawing, but you have to write well." In fact, Denzel believes that you could say that drawing too well could be a liability. There are too many cartoonists who can make beautiful drawings, but they don't have very much to say. He notes that everybody tends to imitate the style of those who succeed. His assessment of his drawing is that it is just so-so. He repeats that if you want to succeed in this business, you've got to know about a lot; you've got to read, go to the movies, watch TV, and develop interests and a natural curiosity for what's going on all over the world.

Profile: Professor and Former Disney Producer and Animator

James, an animator/cartoonist, worked for Disney Studios for eighteen years as a producer-director and now teaches several college-level courses in film production, editing, and animation. One of those courses is called Animation 2, which is about storyboarding specifically for animation. He has also taught a course in Animation Production Studios.

James notes that even with the increased use of the computer in animation, you still have to have the drawing and the storyboarding skills. You need to know about such things as composition and light. But the computer has greatly impacted the industry, he says. *Toy Story*, for instance, was done entirely by computer—even the little boy and his mother, the main live characters, were created by the computer. Another big use of the computer, he notes, is in stop-motion animation. Using the computer makes the camera work much simpler. He says that beginning animators get a year or so to learn drawing and traditional computer skills and another year or so to learn individual programs.

Not everyone has to have the same kinds of drawing skills that would be necessary to get a drawing job at Disney, he advises, suggesting that if you look at many of the cartoon shows on TV on Saturday morning, they have a different kind of animation. A lot of animation is done for video games. It's a simpler kind of animation at this point, he notes, but it's a growing field. He finds that the demand is for good, creative people who are able to work well with other people.

James recognizes that it's a collaborative enterprise to produce animated films. Hundreds of people are involved in producing animated features, he says. Different people write the script, compose and score the music, handle sound effects, and more. For example, layout people work closely with the director of the film. They take the storyboards and actually compose the shots and backgrounds that will be used for animation. They don't necessarily create the backgrounds or the characters, he points out—others do that.

"Animators are in demand right now," he says, "but the market is like any other. As more and more people get into the field, the competition becomes fiercer. Animation is part show business, which can be very erratic. It still takes exceptional talent and self-motivation to do well."

4

What It Takes

It's been stated before in this book, but it bears repeating: cartooning is not for everyone. In fact, it's not for most people. It takes a unique mix of talent, persistence, and the cartooning itch to make it in this field. So if you want a job where you know what to expect from day to day, where the hours are fairly uniform and the pay is steady—cartooning is probably not for you. Although the rewards can be great, especially if your cartoon strip is syndicated and runs in hundreds of papers in the United States and Canada, it's a field that's very hard to break into. The competition is keen and becoming keener, and few have the talent to succeed. Even talent does not automatically spell success. Now animation—that's an entirely different matter. Here the work is much more available. You still need talent and many other skills, but the odds are much better that you can find a job if you do have what it takes.

Cartooning Itch

What do we mean when we refer to the cartooning itch? We mean that you must have the intense desire to succeed more than anything else. As John McPherson, creator of *Close to Home* put it: "To succeed in cartooning, you have to want it bad enough." To further illustrate, he said that if he won the lottery, he'd still be cartooning, because he loves what he does. And chances are what is true of McPherson holds true of just about every other cartoonist. The itch to create shows itself early on, in childhood, and with it you can climb mountains. You will have the strength to persist no matter what. To support yourself, you may have to work outside the field as an illustrator for an advertising agency or video-game producer or do layouts for an art studio. Or you may have to work as a waiter, dishwasher, or bricklayer—anything to make a living. And you may have to confine your cartooning to your spare time, including weekends, evenings, and even holidays. The point is that you must love cartooning so much that you will do whatever it takes to succeed. With that kind of attitude, you just might make it.

Drawing and Writing Talent

The itch may help to keep you going in the face of adversity, but it can get you just so far. You still must have one indispensable quality to succeed, and that is talent in drawing. Okay, you don't have to be a Rembrandt or a Botticelli, but you must be able to draw objects realistically enough that readers will be able to recognize them instantly. Your cartoons must be able to stand pretty much on their own, with perhaps a few strategically placed words of explanation. As Chris Browne, who has done the *Hagar the Horrible* cartoon strip for many years, puts it: "The best thing any aspiring cartoonist can do . . . is to learn the basics of drawing in addition to reading books on the subject." It's a good idea to take a drawing class (see "Educational Requirements" later in this chapter). Cartooning may seem hard at first, he continues, but it's important to learn as much about the basics as possible.

Although the drawing skills are probably the most natural part of the art, you must also have the ability to write clearly and succinctly—that is, with as few words as possible. Bill Amend, creator of the comic strip *Fox Trot*, finds the writing to be the most natural part of creating a cartoon, so he spends the bulk of his time on the drawing to reflect what he wants to say. It comes down to this: your writing must be easily read and understood, and it should convey your message in as little space as possible. This is not so easy to do. *Beetle Bailey*'s originator, Mort Walker, says readers will give your strip no more than seven seconds. If it looks like it will be too hard to understand or if there are too many words to read, they will just skip it.

Point of View

In addition to possessing the talent and the itch to succeed, there is one more necessary element that you must have to make it in cartooning, and that is a point of view or style that reflects your personality. You've got to be completely honest. As one cartoonist put it, cartooning is you—it's personal and shows your personality.

So how do you do this? How do you develop a style that reflects who you are and what you stand for? The answer is not so simple: You've got to be a student of human nature. You've got to understand what makes people tick and know what's happening in the world—fashion, sports, new trends, current events, and hot topics.

Read everything you can lay your hands on. Keep up with the news as dispersed through the media—books, newspapers, magazines, and anything that reflects what's going on in the world at large. Set aside some time to watch TV and go to the movies, because both of these media reflect society—the way we look, act, talk, and what turns us on. This is the fodder that you as the cartoonist must polish and transform into something that rings a bell with your readers. As one cartoonist put it: "Read a lot, watch a lot of TV, travel, suffer, take life-drawing classes, visit museums, find a job on a weekly newspaper, and hope for the big time. And hold on to your day job!"

It has even been suggested by one or two cartoonists that skill in drama or acting can help. You're not trying to be a movie star, but such skills will help you understand human nature and know how to tap the emotions of your viewers or readers.

One other quality you need—and this should be fairly obvious—is a good sense of humor. Ordinarily, this is something that is inherent—either you have it or you don't. But it wouldn't do any harm to study some of the great comedians of the past, such as Bob Hope, Jack Benny, and Gracie Allen, and current stars such as Jay Leno, David Letterman, Jim Carrey, Chris Rock, and Jon Stewart. Find out what their audience finds funny, what works for them and what doesn't. It may not work for you, but it's something to start with, and you can work at it until you polish your own approach to what's funny as reflected in your cartoons.

Character Development

The late and great cartoonist, Charles M. Schulz, who created *Peanuts*, reportedly said that before you do anything, you must develop some unique and outstanding characters such as those in *Doonesbury, Beatle Bailey*, and *Mr. Boffo*. Very few will remember the words we write, he said, but they will remember the personalities of the characters we draw and what they looked like. Such characters must spring from our own personalities, our own experiences, and our own views. Often, successful comic strip characters will become more real to the reader than real life as they laugh, cry, and show anger or contentment. Over the years we have seen them develop, as in *Gasoline Alley, For Better or For Worse*, and, of course, in *Little Orphan Annie*.

How do we create memorable characters? Well, there are really unlimited ways of doing this. But many successful cartoonists have found inspiration in their own back yards. *Dennis the Menace*, for instance, sprang into real life when cartoonist Hank Ketcham learned that his wife called their son Dennis "the menace."

The characters that make up Bill Keane's *Family Circus* were all based on members of his family. Animator Walter Lantz, who created Woody Woodpecker, modeled this famed character after a pesky woodpecker that kept bothering him and his bride during their honeymoon. *Hagar the Horrible* was the name trumped up for cartoonist Dik Browne by his sons. If you read this cartoon strip, you know that Hagar's horned helmet, rough beard, and shaggy tunic make him look somewhat like a caveman or a primitive Viking, but you also know that Hagar has a soft underbelly that is exposed from time to time.

Getting over Rough Spots

There are times when even the most successful cartoonists draw a complete blank as to what they want to draw or say. But you can't let writer's block or a creative dry spell get you down. You simply have to work your way out of it until you are once again producing. If your strip is syndicated, you know that you have to produce a certain number of strips, come hell or high water, as the expression goes. As one syndicate bigwig put it: "You have to produce week in and week out, and you have to consistently produce good work. You can't be the sort of person where, when you experience highs, you turn out good work, and when you go through down periods, you have nothing to show for your efforts."

Cartooning, especially comic strip cartooning, is a discipline. Often you must work doubly hard to overcome periods when you run into a creative block. It may take several efforts, but eventually you will start clicking and find your niche. Chic Young, the originator of *Blondie,* had problems thinking of a subject that seemed to work before he clicked with *Blondie* many years ago. These keys to cartooning success also apply to animators.

Educational Requirements

As Mike Keane, editorial cartoonist of the *Denver Post,* puts it: "Because editorial cartooning is such an odd mix of history, politics, art, writing, and humor, all college subjects are valuable for the beginning cartoonist. Study each of them as part of a curriculum you will need."

Keane also has this to say about cartooning education. "If you have the talent, the ability to produce daily, you have the same credentials required of your colleagues in journalism. There are some cartoonists . . . who did not go to college. But they are in the distinct minority. You will need a résumé and a grade-point average that reflects a dedication to the subjects you will use every day at the drawing board."

Like Keane, most cartoonists agree that a broad liberal arts background is best, and, surprisingly, most caution against art school. However, if an art school also provides a broad-based liberal arts program, including music, drama, political science, science, and history, that would be very helpful. It's a good idea to take at least one drawing course somewhere along the line, so that you can learn to draw more realistically, even though cartooning is by nature exaggerated and unrealistic. Who has seen an actual human with the overblown arms that characterize a cartoon character like Popeye?

Fortunately, there are many schools in the United States and Canada that offer formal cartooning programs (see Appendix D). Among them and perhaps the most prominent is Joe Kubert's School of Cartoon and Graphic Arts in Dover, New Jersey, which offers a three-year program in film animation and cartooning. It is taught by respected professionals and graduates who have found jobs in comic books, syndication, and greeting cards with leading companies such as Disney Studios, Hallmark, and Marvel Comics. As one successful graduate put it, "The course load was unbelievable, but it really prepares you to meet deadlines and improves your artistic ability much more than you could do on your own. Also, even though it emphasizes comic book art, we were well trained in other areas such as the human figure, advertising, method, and materials." Another highly respected school is New York City's School of Visual Arts. Here, some pros have been teaching for more than fifty years.

In animation, the program is considerably different, with many schools that are highly recommended (see Appendix D). Most of these schools offer courses in both traditional and computer-assisted animation. The key to animation remains the story and the animator's ability to tell the story in a way that touches the viewer. To the basic story the animator must add the elements of humor, drama, and other emotions that really stir us. But since the technical part of animation, and especially computer graphics, is so prominent today, it is a very good idea that you enroll in a program that offers a degree in fine arts, film or video, or animation.

You need an overall idea of what is involved in the animation process, including how you account for the passage of time on film or how many frames to allot for any given action of your characters. You must also be able to take apart a scene piece by piece and frame by frame. Understanding the parts is the formula for understanding the whole. Four-year programs are the norm, although a few programs are three years.

Tuition can run quite high, ranging from about $10,000 to $20,000 a year, excluding room and board and books. Fortunately, most schools offer financial aid in the form of federal and state loans, scholarships, and work-study programs. When researching these programs, you will certainly want to look into the kinds and levels of financial assistance offered.

Although the California Institute of Arts (Cal Arts) is perhaps the most prestigious school for studying animation, it is also one of the hardest to get into. Nearly all of the schools listed in Appendix D offer the background training and technical courses you will need to work in animation today, whether at one of the big Hollywood studios, such as Disney, Hanna-Barbera, or Universal, or at one of the many production studios located throughout the United States and Canada. Such smaller studios do a lot of the work for television commercials and special effects and much more.

Keep in mind that, increasingly, community colleges are offering courses in basic animation and computer graphics and video production. To ensure a place in any of these programs, as well as in the other schools listed in Appendix D, you must register early. Ordinarily, community college programs offer basic courses that are more affordable and more accessible than the three- and four-year programs. The programs offered in community colleges provide an introduction to computer graphics, but you may want to consider going on to some of the other schools listed because they offer more advanced computer graphics and imaging equipment.

If you are interested in applying for a position with Disney, note that Disney and other major studios welcome submissions from anyone in their final year of college or with a degree from any accredited college or university. Contact Disney Animation Training for additional details at: Walt Disney Feature Animation, 2100 Riverside Drive, Burbank, California 91506.

For less formal training in animation or cartooning, contact a local art museum to see if it offers any cartooning courses. You might also consider taking a correspondence course. One that is highly recommended is Cartoonerama, a twenty-four lesson course covering every phase of cartoon art. For more information, contact Cartoonerama, P.O. Box 248, Chalfont, Pennsylvania 18414. Its website is cartooncrossroads.com. Many books also offer lessons in cartooning, and several of these are listed in the Further Reading section at the back of the book. Many of these even offer personal feedback on your work. Usually covered is a variety of areas, including how to draw faces, bodies, hands, and feet; motion; background; perspective; and a good deal more.

What else can you do to learn something about cartooning? Obviously, you should study the masters, and there is no better way to start than to subscribe to the local paper and start reading the comics every day. Read cartoon books to learn what makes these collections so successful. Read all kinds of comic books—those whose humor tends to be dark or sarcastic, like *Sylvia* by Nicole Hollander or Bud Grace's *Ernie*, or whose humor is more gentle and family oriented, such as Lynn Johnston's *For Better or For Worse*.

Profile: Greeting Card and Comic Strip Cartoonist

Michael says that he had always loved cartooning but never thought of making a career of it. In college, he did a few political cartoons for the campus newspaper. After working in an office and trying to make a living as a street vendor, he thought he would try his luck at drawing cartoons. He did that for a year or so before being offered a job working part-time as a graphic designer for a record company. Since it was an appealing offer, he moved and took the job. Even at that time, he worked hard to build his cartooning business, which is now his main source of income.

There are quite a few cartoonists who do cartoons for greeting card companies. But Michael finds that his work seems to be too far-out for most greeting card companies, so he has been creating them mostly on his own. Besides creating greeting cards, he does a syndicated panel once a week and has written several books. He has also compiled collections of his best cartoons and has had several books published to date.

His time is evenly distributed between his greeting card business, the panel that he does weekly for syndication, and the books that he has been working on, as well as the cartoons that he submits regularly for various magazines. "I probably spend more time thinking of ideas for new cartoons, but the greeting card business occupies a lot of my time," he says. "So you can see that it is quite a hodgepodge of assignments."

Although he has always had an artistic flair, he has never received an art education. But he recognizes that a good many cartoonists have gone to art schools like the Art Institute in Chicago, and he regrets not going to school there. He believes that this might have helped him considerably, because he finds that style is largely dependent on the artist's limitations, and he admits that he's not a good artist. "Training in the arts will help, obviously," he says, "although you can get by without it, and many cartoonists have done just that."

Michael notes that a few places in the country offer specific training for cartoonists, such as the College of Visual Arts in New York (see Appendix D), but there aren't too many. After completing college, he took a course in gags and humor and another in designing and marketing at a school in California—the California College of Arts and Crafts. Both of these courses were worthwhile because they helped him avoid a few years of hard knocks. The valuable lessons he learned could otherwise have taken him many years of trial and error.

"Testing your suitability for this career is hit and miss," he says. "If you think your work is funny, then by all means give it a shot." In his case, it was mostly luck and perseverance that worked. He advises that you should first try to get your cartoons published in as many places as possible—the high school paper, the yearbook, and the flyers that are produced in school. If no one understands what you're trying to do, then you might as well forget about it, he says.

He also recommends that you not overlook magazines. Many magazines publish clever gag or panel cartoons, and they are not all in the consumer field. There are many specialty magazines, such as *Linoleum Monthly*, *Steel Age*, and so forth, that use good cartoons.

And then there are pet magazines such as *Cat Fancy*, *Dog Fancy*, and *Bird Fancy*.

If you are interested in a particular aspect of cartooning—humorous illustration, greeting cards, political cartoons—he notes that there's a magazine for aspiring cartoonists that can be very helpful. *Cartoonists Profiles* is published in Connecticut and runs many interviews with cartoonists and others in the field, including syndicators and magazine editors.

Another magazine that Michael enjoys reading is *Comics Journal*, which specializes in cartooning. He finds it great in explaining how other cartoonists get their ideas and how they get started. It's really inspiring, he comments, since they come from all walks of life and all parts of the country, but they all share a fundamental belief that cartooning is something that they have to do. This is what they've always wanted to do, and they would not be happy doing anything else.

Profile: Director of Animation in a College Film Department

Alejandro teaches at a college in Chicago and is part of the film and video department. He says that the department's philosophy is that you need to be a traditional animator before you can be a computer animator, sand animator, cutout animator, or anything else. The school runs its students through a very intensive two-year program that covers history, basic skills, storytelling skills, training, and motion before they can actually get into studying computer animation.

He notes that computers have opened up many possibilities in the field. There's a major misconception among students that in animation you really don't have to know how to draw. That's why they want to get into computer animation. But, he says, the school's philosophy is that the computer is a tool, not the means itself.

Once the students understand the art of storytelling, storyboarding, character design, timing, sound, history, and figure drawing, they are instructed in applying these elements to an original story. In their last two years, students spend most of their time working on their own material and trying to get their portfolios together. The school tries to balance the course work, working not only with computers but also with sand animation, clay animation, and cutouts.

You can take traditional animation and scan it into the computer and digitally paint it, so there are no more brushes and paints. "The analogy I use for my students is that it's like an electron microscope," he says. "What can you see, now that you have this wonderful high-power microscope? You can see things that nobody has seen before.

"In computer animation we can create—using mathematical processes—the real world and then fly through it," he continues. "We can go inside walls and inside watches. And the computer allows us to do things that you could never imagine. Computer photos start very large, and then they are electrophotographically reduced to microscopic size."

Alejandro notes that animation is a field where if you have the talent and you really want to do it, the sky's the limit. Several of his school's graduates are working at Disney, for example, and they love doing it.

Even with the demand for those high-tech skills, he says, there is still a large market for those with traditional animation skills. Similar to the predictions that the computer would cut down on the need for paper and that television was going to completely replace the radio—both of which have yet to come true—animators' talents are still necessary to the process of producing animated films. Even though computers are a necessary part of the process of creating animated films, the entertainment industry itself is really based on your audience's likes and dislikes. Audiences get bored very easily, he cautions, so you always have to come up with new ideas, and that can only be done with a living, breathing human being.

Alejandro finds that the major benefit of employing computers instead of manpower is that they can dramatically cut down on production time. Although he doesn't know what the cost difference is in developing a feature using computers as compared to traditional animation, he would be surprised if there was much of a difference at all. Both are expensive, primarily because of the many hours of work required to do the job.

He also says that the market is both commercially oriented and feature-entertainment oriented and that you really cannot separate the two. The educational market is a big one, and within that market there are submarkets, including religious markets and others.

One of the things that students learn, he says, is that the field is very competitive. Talent, punctuality, solid work habits, commitment, and love of the media are traits that you must possess to succeed. There are many easier ways to make a living. According to him, if you don't love it, you really should look for employment elsewhere.

To see if you are right for cartooning, he says, you should first of all like drawing, and he offers several questions that you should ask yourself when considering this field: Have you enjoyed drawing all of your life? Did you grow up doodling on any and all pieces of paper within your reach? Did you create cartoons for your high school newspaper? (In his case, he didn't enjoy history very much, but he could summarize it in a cartoon strip!) Do you enjoy working with your hands? Do you love to be creative? Do you enjoy challenges? It's very much of an individual effort, he says, until you get to the production level, and then you must be a team player. All members of the team have to pull their own weight and have the talent to make each part of the process work to make the whole run smoothly. The collective love for what you all are doing is the bottom line.

Alejandro finds that the creativity involved in starting from scratch is challenging and demanding. Technologically, he says, you have to be savvy. You have to be able to change your styles constantly. Animation involves the best of many arts—the fine arts, filmmaking, computer technology, and others.

Everyone is born with different talents, personalities, and points of view, he notes. Drawing has styles, and approaches can vary. He gives the example of Tim Burton, who's a terrific animator. But it took him ten years to get his foot in the door at Disney to make his stop-motion film *The Nightmare Before Christmas*, a movie that is truly wonderful and definitely has the stamp of individuality.

5

GETTING STARTED

BECOMING A PROFESSIONAL cartoonist or animator is not an easy thing to do, as has already been noted in this book. But one good thing about cartooning is that your options are very broad. Creating cartoons for magazines; having your cartoon strip syndicated; illustrating children's books; illustrating greeting cards and calendars; working for an advertising agency; doing animation for various production houses throughout the United States and Canada; teaching animation either part-time or full-time in community colleges, art schools, and other schools of the fine and graphic arts; and working in one of the major studios, such as Disney, Dream-Works, Universal, or Warner Bros., are just a few of the fields that you can explore. Read some of the interviews in this book, and you probably will find other options to look into also.

But get this straight: very few cartoonists go right from school into a full-time job in cartooning. Most get jobs in advertising agencies or art and layout studios as illustrators and graphic arts designers, or with book and magazine publishers as illustrators and layout designers. Others start out in any number of jobs as waiters, sales-people, and so forth, just to have some income while they strive to get started as cartoonists and animators. As has previously been stressed, you may have to work evenings, weekends, and holidays for cartooning. If you have a husband or wife who works, you may even have to live off of one income for a while until you get established as a cartoonist or animator.

Newspapers Versus Magazines

As has already been stated, the market for newspaper comic strips has shrunk rapidly in recent years, and as one cartoonist put it, it takes so long to become established that anyone under forty is probably working a second job or creating cartoons only in his or her spare time. You may find yourself juggling comic strips, freelance graphic arts design, editorial panels, headline design, and more. Many cartoonists recommend starting out by submitting panel cartoons or gags to magazines and special-interest publications of all sorts. This is probably the best way to see if you have the thick skin necessary to withstand the rejection slips that will almost certainly come your way, especially in the beginning. Unfortunately, this seems to be the lot of almost all cartoonists, even those who are well-established. This can also be a good barometer of how much you enjoy cartooning. If you attain any degree of success at it, you can go on to loftier and more demanding projects, such as pitching comic book publishers on a comic book idea or trying your luck in having your cartoon strip syndicated. This will take considerably more time and energy than submitting a few gag cartoons to a magazine, but the magazine market is certainly a good way to test the waters.

Beating the Rejection Blues

As you strive to get started, you must learn to get used to having your work rejected. It could take years before you make your first sale, and this is not necessarily a reflection on you. Tom Cheney, a cartoonist who has had his work accepted by the *New Yorker*, the *Saturday Evening Post*, and other publications, says: "I don't think rejections are a valid judge of a cartoonist's work. Cartoons get rejected for thousands of trivial reasons in a market that changes like the weather." To ease the pain of rejection, Cheney asks himself why he got into the business in the first place. His reply: "I love to draw, I love writing . . . and I can't think of anything else that I'd rather be doing." Cheney ought to know. He spent two painful years receiving rejection slips until he made his first cartoon sale to the *Saturday Evening Post*. Within a year, he sold another cartoon to the *New Yorker*. Soon more and more magazines were accepting his work until he was able to go full-time as a freelancer, one of the "scariest" decisions he has ever made.

Luann's Greg Evans started submitting cartoon strips to syndicates while he was in college, in 1970, and worked at it for ten years on and off before *Luann* hit in 1980. More than once, he admits, he was ready to throw in the towel, but, as he puts it: "As anyone who carries the cartooning virus will tell you, you can't get rid of it. It's a lifelong affliction."

Courting Ideas

Undoubtedly one of the hardest aspects of being a cartoonist/animator is getting ideas. That is, it's hard to come up with ideas that are fresh, meaningful, and have something to say to today's cartoon strip reader. If you were to survey a dozen of today's leading cartoonists as to how and where they get their ideas—the lifeblood of their work—chances are you'd get a dozen different replies.

Tom Cheney finds that the late hours of the evening and the wee hours of the morning work best for him. This is apt to be the period when the house is the quietest and when there are the fewest interruptions. John Caldwell finds that riding an exercise bike for about forty-five minutes each morning works best for him. While he rides, he also reads the newspaper or a book or magazine and tries to derive inspiration from something that he has picked up in the course of his reading. Bud Grace, *Ernie's* creator, likes to go for long two-hour walks every day. He claims that he's always walked to get the creative juices flowing—plus, for someone who spends most of his time at the drawing board, it gives him some exercise. *Broom-Hilda's* Russell Myers likes to start out reading the funnies to get him in the mood. For him, coming up with gags is not so tough; the problem is finding some subject materials upon which to hang the gag. Some cartoonists carry a small, handheld tape recorder around with them at all times of the day and tape thoughts for gags as they get them.

One of the most common approaches is that of *Beetle Bailey's* Mort Walker, who simply starts writing to see where it will take him. For example, you could write down words like "cash to money to funds," and so forth, repeatedly until inspiration strikes. Some cartoonists doodle or sketch. Some experiment with taking a simple sketch of, say, a pencil and seeing how *it* can be converted into an airplane with the addition of a few simple lines. Continue this exercise in creativity until an idea pops up. Another tactic that works for many is to take another cartoonist's work and with a few deft strokes turn it into something entirely different. But the free-form principle is still the key. Take something simple, add a few lines and twists, and see where it takes you. You can see that there are many ways you can get into the cartooning mindset, many of which revolve around following a set routine every day—fishing for ideas at a certain time of the day or night, exercising both body and mind, and reading daily newspapers, magazines, funnies, or comic books.

But what do you do if, despite following these guidelines to the letter, you find yourself running dry—what is referred to in the profession as *writer's block*? This happens to all cartoonists at one time or another. You try this approach and that one, but nothing seems to work. When this happens to you, try to break the routine. Visit a friend, go to the aquarium, or any museum for that matter, or a local floral garden, watch a movie, read a book—in short, try to recharge your batteries. Relax and don't even think about cartooning. This should help jump-start your creative powers.

Many Ways to Skin a Cat

To see how many successful cartoonists broke into the field, let's examine what they did to get started. Steve Barr is a professional cartoonist who has launched a syndicated comic strip, done panel and gag cartoons, and designed and illustrated board games (bet you didn't think of this option), books, and educational materials. He has worked in animation, illustration, and advertising. His first recollection of drawing a cartoon was in the fourth grade, when he copied a sketch of Mickey Mouse onto his desk. After being lectured by his teacher—who made him clean the drawing off the desk and informed him that drawings should be done on sheets of paper, not furniture—she told him that his work was good and suggested that he enter the school art contest, which he did and won.

From that day on, Steve knew that he wanted to become a professional cartoonist. He spent hours in the local library reading everything that he could dig up on cartooning. He bombarded famous cartoonists with letters, begging them to share their secrets with him. Many sent wonderful letters with all kinds of helpful hints. He locked himself in his room practicing sketching and trying out various pens, paper, and ink until he was fairly certain that he was ready to become a cartoonist.

He sold his first two cartoons to a magazine and a newspaper syndicate when he was in the seventh grade. For his labors, he received two checks—one for seven dollars and the other for twenty-five dollars. Steve was on his way. By the time he was in high school, he was being published regularly by several magazines. In the course of those early days in his career, Steve's mother had a four-drawer filing cabinet of rejection slips that he received over the years, but he never gave up. He remembers the words of a friend in the business, who'd told him that to succeed as a cartoonist he'd have to persist and he'd have to keep doing what he was doing over and over again. And that's what Barr did. He tried over and over. In his words: "If you have created cartoons worth printing, some editor somewhere will eventually find your talent."

Lynn Johnston's path to success was both roundabout and long. For her first job, she worked in a Vancouver animation studio inking and painting cels. Later, she freelanced, handling everything from typesetting to designing cereal boxes, posters, flyers, and book illustrations. In 1972, while pregnant with her first child, she created eighty cartoons about pregnancy that were published in a book entitled *David, We're Pregnant*. To her amazement, the book sold three hundred thousand copies. That was the trigger that caused United Press Syndicate to offer her a contract on her new strip, *For Better or For Worse*.

Roz Chast, one of the *New Yorker*'s top cartoonists, combines her career as a cartoonist with homemaking. She got her start in 1978, about a year after graduating from the Rhode Island School of Design, when several of her cartoons were picked up by a few off-beat or alternative publications like the *National Lampoon* and the *Village Voice*. From there it was but a short step to the *New Yorker*, where she has been a mainstay ever since. On top of that, she has had eight books of her cartoon collections published in addition to freelancing for advertising agencies and corporations.

Jerry Craft, originator of the *Mama's Boyz* strip, attributes much of his success to a website that he designed himself. He cautions that for every overnight success in cartooning—such as *Mutts*, *Dilbert*, or *Zits*—thousands of cartoonists are plugging along trying to hit the jackpot. Even if a syndicate turns you down, you should never give up. Craft's cartoon characters are now being featured on computer mouse pads, and he is in negotiations to license his characters to several greeting card companies and animation studios.

Want more success stories? How about John McPherson, the creator of *Close to Home*. McPherson worked for years as an engineer before deciding to try his hand at cartooning. After a full day at the office, he would rush home and work at cartooning well into the evening. It was a passion—an obsession—that eventually paid off when he sold some of his work to a religious-oriented publication. Eventually, he wound up with a contract for worldwide syndication and book rights by Universal Press Syndicate.

Then there was Jared Lee, who worked for years as an advertising illustrator, numbering among his clients Ralston Purina, the U.S. Postal Service, John Deere, and Sunkist. At the same time, he had considerable luck in having his panel cartoons accepted by such magazines as the *Saturday Evening Post*, *Cosmopolitan*, *Woman's Day*, and *Playboy*. He was also doing illustrations for greeting cards for

Hallmark and Gibson Greetings. Eventually, he hit pay dirt with the publication of the book *A Hippopotamus Ate the Teacher*. That was the springboard for a very successful career in children's book illustration.

So what it amounts to is that there is no one path to success in cartooning. Most likely you will have to work at a combination of jobs in this field involving book illustration, greeting cards, comic books, and magazine gags before you can land in one of the higher paying markets, such as comic strip syndication or illustrating children's books. It will take lots of work and perhaps years of patience and a stiff upper lip, but it can be done if you have the talent and the persistence to keep trying.

An Open Field

Both animation and cartooning are fields that are open to anyone with talent. Sex, age, and race are not barriers. Women have found that the doors to success open just as wide for them as they do for men. Besides Nicole Hollander and Roz Chast, among the cartoon newcomers are Hilary Price, who at age twenty-six was the youngest cartoonist in daily newspaper syndication when her strip *Rhymes with Orange* was launched in 1995. The strip, which deals with everything from body piercing to dating problems, now appears in more than one hundred newspapers coast to coast. Julie Larson's *The Dinette Set* started appearing in alternative newspapers in 1990 and was picked up by King Features Syndicate six years later. Today it appears in more than one hundred daily papers in the United States. Other famed women cartoonists with long-time running cartoon strips are Lynn Johnston (*For Better or For Worse*) and Dale Messick (*Brenda Starr: Reporter*).

The boom in animation and the resulting need for new talent makes that field particularly barrier-free.

How Pay Is Figured

It is estimated that six out of ten cartoonists are freelancers whose pay and hours are subject to the availability of work. This is not as true of animators, who work for feature films and TV productions, where the work can run for longer periods of time and the pay is more regular. But ordinarily freelancers work when a job is available. Although the hours are fairly stable, there are times when you are working against a deadline and where you may have to work nights, weekends, and even holidays to complete the job on time.

There are also periods where you may not have any work, especially when you start out in this field. Ordinarily, cartoonists whose work is syndicated are on a more regular schedule. They know that they are responsible for a certain number of comic strips per week and how many hours per week are involved to turn out the work.

Earnings—What You Can Expect

Although the Bureau of Labor Statistics, which is the most reliable source of statistics on earnings, does not list any figures on earnings for cartoonists and animators, an informal survey of those employed in this area revealed the following ballpark figures. There may well be wide deviations from these figures in various parts of the country, and remember that these are gross earnings from which you have to deduct such expenses as cost of living, advertising, insurance, rent, computer graphics software, business travel, and office equipment such as fax machines, photocopiers, and scanners.

As a magazine cartoonist working a few hours each night and weekends, you might earn as little as $50 to as much as $1,000 or more a month. The higher figure would most certainly be true of a seasoned pro who has hundreds or thousands of cartoons in circulation. A few magazines might pay as little as $5 per cartoon, but most pay between $50 and $500 for each single-panel cartoon published. Working full-time as a magazine cartoonist, your earnings could fluctuate between $2,000 and $4,500 per month. Most magazine cartoonists supplement their incomes with earnings derived from doing freelance work for advertising, greeting cards, calendars, children's books, and miscellaneous art for such products as mugs and T-shirts.

Illustrators doing humorous art can be either starving artists or can earn $200,000 a year or higher, because fees paid for magazine illustrations tend to be higher than those paid for cartoons. These can range from $200 for a color illustration for a small magazine to $1,500 or more for an ad an agency places. A greeting card illustration might earn $300, while a calendar project could pay as much as $5,000, spread out over a few years.

Comic book artists are usually paid by the page, a sum that depends somewhat on the magazine and the cartoonist's status. As you might expect, beginners tend to produce fewer pages a month and earn much less than the pros, who work faster and produce more pages.

Full-time staff artists for greeting card companies can expect to earn between $300 and $600 per week, depending on experience, length of employment, and the size of the company.

Political cartoonists, on the other hand, earn roughly the same salaries as editors and publishers, which range from approximately $30,000 to $60,000 a year, depending on length of service and the size of the newspaper. However, if your work is sold to other papers by a syndicate, you can expect to earn additional royalties, depending on the number and size of the papers using your cartoons.

By far the greatest earnings jackpot you can expect to hit as a newspaper strip cartoonist is through syndication. Again, the market is becoming increasingly tough to crack, but if you are one of the lucky few, you can expect to see your earnings soar to between $60,000 to $150,000 a year if the strip is carried by at least three hundred newspapers. Unfortunately, the number of cartoonists in this bracket continues to dwindle, and several well-known artists must hold down day jobs while devoting evenings and weekends to strips as a protection against the possibility of having their strip canceled by the syndicate.

In the field of animation, a recent survey revealed the salaries of those working in forty-five job titles. A representative sampling of those titles and the median earnings of each follows:

Producer	$208,000
Art director	$153,000
Director	$109,200
Character animator	$106,000
Staff writer	$103,000
Effects animator	$101,000
Background layout artist	$91,000
Background painter	$89,400
Staff production member	$88,400
Color key/color stylist	$62,500
Effects assistant	$61,200
Apprentice trainee	$42,700
In-betweener	$42,300

As you can see, there is quite a range between the jobs shown here—and remember, these are median figures. Many earn much less than the amounts shown here and many considerably more.

As is true of cartoonists, total earnings will reflect your experience, your status in the industry, and the size and location of the firm you work for.

Pros and Cons of a Cartooning Career

Although there is admittedly a lot of risk and very little security in launching a career in cartooning, there are other payoffs besides money if your strip is picked up by a syndicate. For one, you are your own boss and can determine when you want to work and what subjects you want to cover. You can be as casual as you want in your clothes and appearance, since in most cases you will be working out of your own studio. And you may spend little if any time commuting to and from work. This can be a big consideration if you have a family and if you are tired of the constraints of reporting to work every day of the workweek.

But then there are the costs of setting up your own studio and investing in office furniture, computers, scanners, and everything else you will need to get started. Also, you will not be entitled to any of the job benefits that you would ordinarily receive as a full-timer working for a company, such as paid holidays and vacations, hospitalization, and life and health insurance. Unless you have a full-time job, you will have to pay for many job benefits yourself.

What Animation Has to Offer

Animation is an entirely different story. If you are considering a career in animation, now is the time to act. The advent of cable and video, as well as the new technology in computer graphics, has generated a whole host of animation marketed to all ages. That means more jobs, so many more people are finding opportunities in animation. What do you have to do to take advantage of these opportunities? For one, you need to give yourself over entirely to your artwork so as to display the full range of your talents and drawing skills. You should understand that the job of animator covers a broad range of positions in the animation process. Explore the many challenging and fulfilling jobs that are part of the industry, such as layout artist, background artist, colorist, and even model builder, to see which most closely matches your skills and aptitudes. Before you even think of going out on an interview, you should have a portfolio bulging with samples of your best artwork and landscapes. If you are interested in model building, you will need to show proof of your talent in three-dimensional work. A sample storyboard or reel showing your best work is what those doing the hiring most often look at. As an alternative, you might consider making an animation short and sending it to various studios you are interested in working for. You might also consider showing your animated short at one of the many film and video festivals that are currently thriving. You can obtain a list of such festivals from the Academy of Motion Picture Arts and Sciences at 8940 Wilshire Boulevard, Beverly Hills, California 90211. Its website is oscars.org.

Opportunities exist all over Canada and the United States to be sure, but the advantage gained by studying in a major animation capital such as Los Angeles are the many internships available to students at all of the major animation studios. If you have at least a little background in animation, this is a great way to combine some practical experience with the opportunity to make some professional contacts. Although Los Angeles may have the edge in the number of internships available, good internship opportunities do exist all over the United States and Canada. Take advantage of them. A limited number of internships, for example, are available from Walt Disney Animation Florida. Internships are described as in-depth work experiences in animation, including instruction, tutorials, practical workshops, studio assignments, and production experience. If selected, you will receive a stipend of at least $285 a week, covering a forty-hour workweek. For information regarding portfolios and résumés, contact Walt Disney Professional Staffing, c/o Animation Division, P.O. Box 10090, Lake Buena Vista, Florida 32820.

Next, you need to do some networking, which is simply making an effort to widen your circle of industry acquaintances. You can do this by joining various animation organizations (some are listed in Appendix B) and by talking to professionals through social events or by working with them on various professional undertakings. And you might even consider interviewing some professionals as a class project. This is yet another good way to get your foot in the door. Finally, explore the work of professionals who preceded you. Read everything you can about the industry. Learn about animation techniques throughout the world from the silent picture era to the present time to see which might work best for you. Some of the film festivals existing today are slanted to avant garde or experimental films. Get to know them to understand the latest techniques influencing the industry today.

Profile: Cartoonist and Illustrator

"Cartooning was something that I had dreamt of doing ever since I was a kid," says Kyle. "I must have started around age six." He recalls tearing pieces of paper in half and then assembling them into comic books. He started to read *MAD* magazine, and this motivated him to pursue cartooning even more. In high school, he submitted work to some of the local papers, and they would occasionally publish a cartoon of his when it dealt with an issue they were interested in. The *Dayton Daily News*, for example, published a series of his cartoons dealing with busing.

He attended St. Clair Community College in Dayton, Ohio, and then enrolled at the Art Institute of Chicago. When he first came to Chicago, he freelanced, doing artwork for small businesses and churches, and he continued with this work until one of his cartoons was published in a Chicago black-community newspaper. He says that he built his freelancing business by calling on various businesses, churches, and other places that the more well-known artists did not care to cultivate. These were businesses that did not have much money to spend, but they still needed artwork to carry on their activities.

Kyle considers the courses that he took at the Art Institute very helpful in the long run. Even though he took courses in animation and art education, he believes that a general education program in any liberal arts school can help in this kind of work. He believes that would-be cartoonists should take specialized courses in addition to their liberal arts classes. For instance, if you want to specialize in political art, he advises that you should take some political courses.

He says that he was interested in comic strips and fell into illustration as part of his interest in editorial cartooning. Currently, he is doing editorial cartoons primarily for weekly and alternative newspapers—those that are not considered part of the mainstream press. Mostly, his cartoons are social commentary in nature, but they often appear on the editorial pages. In Chicago, he does cartoons for a publication widely distributed throughout the city in support of the homeless. His work has appeared in this publication every week for about thirteen years or so. Currently, his cartoons appear in about nine papers, but he'd like to have his work appear in some daily papers—that's his immediate objective. He says that he has approached several syndicates about taking on his work, but he has not had any luck to date.

He also does a good deal of graphic arts—posters, flyers, and layouts—because, as he puts it, he has the computer setup to do this. He considers this work important because it helps pay for his household expenses. Currently, he is splitting his time fifty-fifty between cartooning and the graphic arts, but he would prefer working full-time in cartooning.

While at his last full-time job, working for a youth service agency, Kyle decided that he could do better working for himself. Indeed, he has done fairly well on his own. He had a lot of energy and talked to many people and was able to sell them on publishing several of his comic books—what he terms "social awareness" books. These were distributed through the Chicago Department of Health and the Chicago Board of Education, as well as other boards of education throughout the country and the local Red Cross.

"To succeed in this business," he says, "you must have an appreciation of what is funny. You also need to have a very thick skin, because you are going to face a lot of rejection, which can be very discouraging when you are starting out. You may think you can walk on water, but you will be brought down to earth very quickly in this business." He says that he has been on the fringes of cartooning for a long time because he enjoyed it, but now he feels that he is part of the cartooning field in general, and he doesn't consider it a difficult field to get into.

He cautions that at first you can't expect to make much money in cartooning. Once a comic book is established, however, and gets into the categories of *Spider-Man*, *Batman*, and *Superman*, he says, you can really make some money.

Kyle advises anyone interested in cartooning to take business and accounting in high school. You should also be familiar with the computer and what it can do, since you may wind up being in business for yourself. In addition, he says, you should learn business writing so that you will be able to write professional, polished letters and submit cartoons to various publishers and publications.

6

A GLIMPSE AT THE FUTURE

As ALREADY NOTED in this book, syndication and comic books are where the big payoffs are in this field, but both can take years of determined, hard work as a cartoonist before you make the grade. That's why we stress that realistically your chances of being successful as a cartoonist are better if you have a day job and do cartooning on the side, or if you combine cartooning with graphic arts (lettering and layout design), designing for websites, and so forth. Here is how the market stacks up for aspiring cartoonists.

Newspaper Cartoonists

With more and more metropolitan dailies going out of business or merging with other newspapers, the number of spots open on the comics pages are likewise shrinking. This holds true of openings for editorial or political cartooning in newspapers as well. Unless there is a dramatic rise in the number of papers printed, the market for newspaper cartoonists, unsteady and dropping at best, does not look good. However, it should be noted that while the big city dailies may be on the decline, suburban, weekly, and specialty newspapers are on the rise, and they also purchase cartoons.

Comic Books

Likewise, comic books, after a period of decline, have surged back with the work of such artists as Alex Ross and Frank Miller. Increasingly, comic books are being pitched at adults as well as youngsters. The opportunities for would-be comic book artists and writers look promising.

Magazines

Your best bet in cartooning is to submit sample cartoons to general consumer magazines and to the hundreds of trade or specialty magazines that also buy cartoons. Both markets require originality and talent. Although the payoff is limited, your chances for success are much better in this market. And as noted in Chapter 3, the magazine market can be a door opener to better-paying jobs in a range of fields, including children's book publishing and comic books.

Animation Fast Tracks

Animation is the great hope in the cartooning industry. We have already seen that feature films and TV shows are betting on cartoons to a degree unprecedented in modern times. Disney has risen to new heights, propelled by the success of such animation features as *Lilo and Stitch*, *The Incredibles*, and *Finding Nemo*. The studio is playing up to the renewed interest in animation with the release of more feature films, including *Cars* and *Ratatouille*. Other major studios have new animation features in the works or already released, such as the acclaimed *Happy Feet*, an Australian production released by Warner Brothers. And DreamWorks has committed to produce an animated film of the famed Belgian cartoon character Tintin.

In television, the typical situation comedy has been knocked out by a virtual landslide of new animated cartoons already released or in the works. This is especially true of Fox, which, based on the outstanding success of "The Simpsons," has three new cartoon features in its schedule. Rival networks, including Warner Bros. and UPN, also have animated shows scheduled in their lineups.

You can expect to see renewed emphasis on animated commercials as well. Animation is widely used in video games made for viewing on the TV monitor or on computer screens. These are showing sharp increases in their production in the near future.

Two Successful Animation Schools

As a gauge of where the animation industry is headed, consider the staggering success of Canada's Sheridan College, about a half-hour west of Toronto by train. Founded in 1968 as a fine arts college that offered one course in traditional animation, the school now offers one of the finest college-level fine arts programs in North America and one of the finest animation programs. Sheridan has undoubtedly had the greatest impact in the world of animation. Every year it receives twenty-five hundred applications for its 110 spots. Only about half of the students complete its three-year program, which is often described as ". . . really intense. People are dropping out all of the time because of the workload."

For those who complete the program, the rewards are worth the effort. An estimated twenty-five to forty animation studios send representatives to the school every year to review demonstration tapes and evaluate candidates for hiring. As much as a year before they graduate, Sheridan students capable of doing computer graphics on film are being offered between $50,000 and $75,000 a year, according to Paul Donavan, of Halifax-based Salter Graphics. The Disney producer in charge of *The Hunchback of Notre Dame* estimates that a half dozen Sheridan graduates were among the film's fifty-person animation crew.

An even more dramatic story is that of Rowland High School, located about twenty-five miles south of Hollywood's animation center. The school is home to one of the most innovative animation programs, and it has quietly become the fourth-largest talent supplier to the growing animation industry. About fifty recent graduates now work at Disney Studios, thirty at Warner Bros., and dozens at smaller production houses dotting the entire Los Angeles area. In fact, according to Kim Dunning, a recent graduate who started at Disney for $40,000 a year, this typical entry-level salary rapidly rises to $80,000 and higher per year. Recently the school developed a real-time teleconferencing link with Warner Bros. Through such innovative technology, students can watch the studio's and school's training sessions.

Although these success stories are perhaps a bit extreme, the fact remains that all animation schools are reporting enrollments at all-time highs and similar job offers to graduates. For all of these reasons, it is quite realistic to project that job opportunities will continue to rise for qualified graduates in the years to come.

Profile: Video Editor and Animation Teacher

In addition to teaching animation, Roberta works at a museum as a video editor. When she first transferred to the school as a student, she studied painting and the video arts. Eventually, she became interested in computers and ended up working with computer animation in the arts and technology departments at her college.

She has worked on the computer part of animation, and though she doesn't have the traditional training for animation, she does have some training in film and video. Roberta sees her strengths as being in editing and in computer animation, but not necessarily in character animation. In her three-dimensional animation courses, she feels that the students make wonderful and fantastic narratives and stories.

In working with students, she attempts to find out what's on their minds, what they would like to do, what they are curious about, what experiences they have had, and what's moving them at the moment. She hopes that by the end of the course, they'll each make a short that has some personal meaning to them.

Roberta did some freelance editing for a studio that does character animation for short, thirty-second TV commercials. She notes that it is the job of the animation studio to know exactly what the agency is looking for in terms of content, character, and the look of the animation. Before they actually produce the animation, these companies create drawings and audio to illustrate the commercial's content. While working with this company, she edited some of the rough commercials together, trying to figure out what the timing should be.

There's an item called a *dope sheet* that charts timing for the project, and most of the time it is the producer's or the director's job to fill this out. After you have been doing this for a while, she says, you can estimate the exact timing of the animated project. You then fill out the dope sheet, which is basically a graph of time and the placement of each image at that particular moment. An animator takes the storyboard, which has the dialogue and the main picture, and the dope sheet, which maps out the time, and uses these to create animation that conforms precisely to the producer's expectations.

Roberta has heard of freelance jobs at "The Oprah Winfrey Show," where the artists are making animations that go between the interviews. These jobs pay extremely well, she believes, up to $80 to $90 an hour. The people who fill these positions are trained or have developed skills in aftereffects, which is basically two-dimensional text and video, and in making tiny spots for between interviews.

Several of her students have gone on to Disney Studios. One drawback to these jobs, she says, is that they have to work six days a week, and some days they work long hours. Also, even though Disney offers what seems like a good salary, she cautions when you think about living in Los Angeles and the hours required for the job, it may not be quite as good as you thought.

"We can use the computer to do everything that the camera can do, only more easily, quickly, and inexpensively," she notes. "Computers are very useful in many phases of the production process, including editing and sound, for speeding up a shot, and for keeping things in order. That's what makes animation so incredible. In one computer application, we feed the drawing outlines to a computer, which can then quickly fill in the drawings, instead of hand-painting all of the figures."

She says that many producers know exactly what they want and can conceive of these shots in advance, but there's a whole new generation of people who like to experiment and flip shots around.

The hours in this work are irregular, she warns. Sometimes they are simply nine to five, but many times they are not. Roberta works at the studio three days a week and teaches three days a week. She says that she works six days a week trying to get a lot of experience in various assignments working with various production studios and learning the equipment. She gets home, eats dinner, and perhaps works for another hour or two preparing for class.

When students finish at the school, she notes, they start out with a studio, and they have to be retrained in that studio's procedures. "You don't have to go back to school," she says, "but each job is a little different and involves a period of learning the ropes. It might take a week or two to get used to each job and to learn the vocabulary at that particular studio."

Right now, she says, no animator can know all of the powerful three-dimensional computer-animation programs. Some job listings may call for animators with skill in one particular kind of software, and many times your employer will change from one program to another, so she advises that you have to be flexible: "It's almost impossible to train for a specific computer animation job," she admits.

Major Newspaper Syndicates

FOR SPECIFIC REQUIREMENTS for submitting cartoon panels or strips, write to each syndicate for its guidelines for submission of cartoons.

Canadian Artists Syndicate
Box 429
Mahone Bay, NS 305 2ED
www.artistsyndicate.ca

Cartoonists and Writers Syndicate
67 Riverside Dr., Ste. 1D
New York, NY 10024
www.cartoonweb.com

Chronicle Features
870 Market St.
San Francisco, CA 94102
www.americanchronicle.com

Copley News Service
123 Camino de la Reina
San Diego, CA 92108
www.copleynews.com

Creators Syndicate
5777 W. Century Blvd., Ste. 700
Los Angeles, CA 90045
www.creators.com

King Features Syndicate
300 W. 57th St., 15th Fl.
New York, NY 10019
www.kingfeatures.com

Tribune Media Services
435 N. Michigan Ave., Ste. 1400
Chicago, IL 60611
www.tms.tribune.com

United Feature Syndicate
200 Madison Avenue
New York, NY 10016
www.unitedfeatures.com

United Media
(United Feature Syndicate/NEA)
200 Madison Ave., 4th Fl.
New York, NY 10016
www.unitedmedia.com

Universal Press Syndicate
4520 Main St.
Kansas City, MO 64112
www.uexpress.com

The *Washington Post* Writers Group
1150 15th St. NW
Washington, DC 20071-9200
www.postwritersgroup.com/writersgroup.htm

Organizations

Cartoonist Organizations

Association of American Editorial Cartoonists
3899 N. Front St.
Harrisburg, PA 17111
http://editorialcartoonists.com

An organization that promotes the interests of cartoonists in the United States, Canada, and Mexico

Comic Arts Professional Society
2006 Magnolia Ave.
Burbank, CA 91507
www.capscentral.org

A Los Angeles–based group of cartoonists, writers, and artists working in the comic print media

National Cartoonists Society
1133 Morse Blvd., Ste. 201
Burbank, CA 91507
www.reuben.org

Primary organization covering artists, cartoonists, writers, and others involved in cartooning and animation

Animation Organizations

AMC Siggraph of SE Michigan
P.O. Box 2047
Royal Oak, MI 46068-2047
www.semafx.com

ASIFA is an international organization with thirty branches all over the world, including several in North America, as follows. It stands for Association International du Film d'Animation.

ASIFA Canada
C.P. 5226
Ville St. Laurent, QC H4L 4Z8
www.awn.com/asifa-canada

Canadian chapter of International Animation Society

ASIFA Central
c/o Deanna Morse
School of Communication, Lake Superior Hall
Grand Valley State University
Allendale, MI 49402
www.swcp.com/animate

Midwest chapter of International Animation Society

ASIFA-East (New York)
c/o Michael Sporn Animation
35 Bedford St.
New York, NY 10014
www.asifa.east.com

New York and East Coast branch of those who belong to ASIFA or International Animators Society

ASIFA Hollywood
Antran Manoogian, President
2114 Burbank Blvd.
Burbank, CA 91506
www.asifa-hollywood.org

California nonprofit organization that is devoted to the advancement of animation

Appendix C

Periodicals

Animation Journal
Department of Film and Video
California Institute of the Arts
2700 McBean Pkwy.
Valencia, CA 91355-2397
www.animationjournal.com

Animation Magazine
30941 W. Agoura Rd., Ste. 102
Westlake Village, CA 91361
www.animationmagazine.net

Animation World Magazine
Antics Technology, Inc.
3201 W. 5th St., Ste. F-40
Los Angeles, CA 90017-2019
http://mag.awn.com

The Artist's Magazine
4700 Galbraith Rd.
Cincinnati, OH 45235
www.artistsmagazine.com

Cartoon Brew
www.cartoonbrew.com

Cartoon Cartoons Magazine
www.neymagazine.com

Cartoonnews.com
The Current Events Educational Magazine
www.cartoonnews.com

The Comic Buyer's Guide
705 E. State St.
Iola, WI 54990-0001
www.cbgxtra.com

The Comics Journal
7563 Lake City Way NE
Seattle, WA 98115
www.tcj.com

FPS Magazine of Animation
Frames Per Second
P.O. Box 206
Pierrefonds, QC
Canada H9H 4K9
www.fpsmagazine.com

Gag Recap and *Cartoon Opportunities*
P.O. Box 248
Chalfont, PA 18914

Slate Magazine
www.cartoonbox.slate.com

Toon Magazine
P.O. Box 487
White Plains, NY 10603
www.toonmag.com

Appendix D

Schools

Because schedules, courses, and requirements are subject to change, it is a good idea to contact any school of interest early to get the most up-to-date information.

Cartooning Schools

Academy of Art University
79 New Montgomery St., 4th Fl.
San Francisco, CA 94105-3410
www.academyart.edu

The Art Institute of California–Los Angeles
2900 W. 31st St.
Santa Monica, CA 90400
www.artinstitutes.edu/losangeles

The Art Institute of California–Orange County
3601 W. Sunflower Ave.
Santa Ana, CA 92704-7931
www.artinstitutes.edu/orangecounty

Art Instruction Schools
3400 Technology Dr.
Minneapolis, MN 55418-6000
www.artists-ais.com

Campus Animation
344 Prospect St.
East Orange, NJ 07017
www.campusanimation.com

Cartoon Animation Institute
3440 W. 8th St.
Los Angeles, CA 90005
www.cartoonmation.com

Cartoonerama
P.O. Box 248
Chalfont, PA 18914
www.cartooncrossroads.com

Center for Cartoon Studies
P.O. Box 125
White River Junction, VT 05001
www.cartoonstudies.org

Cogswell Polytechnical College
1175 Bordeaux Dr.
Sunnyvale, CA 94089
www.cogswell.edu

College of Interactive Arts
Interactive Animation
987 Granville St.
Vancouver, BC V6Z 1L3
www.gamercollege.com

Columbia College
600 S. Michigan Ave.
Chicago, IL 60605-1996
www.colum.edu

Columbus College of Art and Design
107 N. Ninth St.
Columbus, OH 43215
www.ccad.edu

Croog Studios
30 W. 26th St., 7th Fl.
New York, NY 10030
www.croogstudios.com/croog.swf

Digital Evolutions–Smoky Hill High School
16100 E. Smoky Hill Rd.
Aurora, CO 80015
www.digital-evolutions.org

Duquesne University
600 Forbes Ave.
Pittsburgh, PA 15282-1702
www.mmtserver.mmt.duq.edu

Earthlight Pictures Animation Training
1332 Kenwood Rd.
Santa Barbara, CA 93109
www.earthlightpictures.com

East Los Angeles College
1301 Avenida Cesar Chavez
Monterey Park, CA 91754-6099
www.ealcart.bizland.com

Edinboro University of Pennsylvania
215 Meadville St.
Edinboro, PA 16444
www.edinboro.edu

Guy Gilchrist's Cartoonist's Academy
237 Hopmeadow St.
Simsbury, CT 06089-9763
www.gillchristcartoonacademy.com

The International Film Workshops
P.O. Box 200
2 Central St.
Rockport, ME 04806
www.theworkshops.com

Joe Kubert School of Cartoon and Graphic Arts
37 Myrtle Ave.
Dover, NJ 07801
kubertsworld.com

Kalamazoo Valley Community College
6767 W. "O" Ave.
P.O. Box 4070
Kalamazoo, MI 49003-4070
www.kvcc.edu

Lake Washington Technical College
11605 132nd Ave. NE
Kirkland, WA 98034-8506
www.lwtc.ctc.edu

M.I.A. Training Center
P.O. Box 172906
Tampa, FL 33602
www.animationtraining.com

Minneapolis College of Art and Design
2501 Stevens Ave. South
Minneapolis, MN 55404
www.mcad.edu

School of the Visual Arts
209 E. 23rd St.
New York, NY 10010
www.schoolofvisualarts.edu

University of Texas at Dallas
P.O. Box 830688
Richardson, TX 75083-0688
www.utdallas.edu

VanArts, Vancouver Institute of Media Arts
837 Beatty St.
Vancouver, BC V6B 2M6
www.vanarts.com

Vancouver Film School
200-198 W. Hastings St.
Vancouver, BC V6B 1H2
www.vfs.com

Virtual Partners Training
1920 Libal St., Ste. 10A
Green Bay, WI 54301
www.virtualpartners.com

Animation Schools

Academy of Art
77 New Montgomery St.
San Francisco, CA 94105
www.academyart.edu

Academy of Digital Animation
Cerro Coso Community College
3000 College Heights Blvd.
Ridgecrest, CA 93555
www.cerrocoso.edu

AI Miami International University of Art and Design
1501 Biscayne Blvd., Ste. 100
Miami, FL 33132
www.artinstitutes.edu/miami

Alfred State College
Computer Arts and Design
Engineering Technology Bldg.
Alfred, NY 14802
www.alfredstate.edu

Algonquin College
Faculty of Arts, Media, and Design
1385 Woodroffe Ave.
Ottawa, ON K2G 1V8
www.algonquincollege.com

Animation Design Center
P.O. Box 751
Lomita, CA 90719
www.animationdesigncenter.com

The Art Center Design College
Animation Graphics
2525 N. Country Club Rd.
Tucson, AZ 85716
www.theartcenter.edu

The Art Institute of Boston at Lesley University
700 Beacon St.
Boston, MA 02215-2599
www.aiboston.edu

The Art Institute of California–Los Angeles
2900 31st St.
Santa Monica, CA 90405
www.artinstitutes.edu/losangeles

Art Institute of Colorado
1200 Lincoln St.
Denver, CO 80203
www.artinstitutes.edu/denver

Art Institute of Philadelphia
1122 Chestnut St.
Philadelphia, PA 19103
www.artinstitutes.edu/philadelphia

Art Institute of Seattle
1323 Elliott Ave.
Seattle, WA 98121-1622
www.artinstitutes.edu/seattle

The Art Institute of Washington
1820 Ft. Meyer Dr.
Arlington, VA 22209-1202
www.artinstitutes.edu/arlington

Art Institutes Online
1400 Penn Ave.
Pittsburgh, PA 15222
www.aionline.edu

Ball State University
Department of Art
Muncie, IN 47206
www.bsu.edu

Bowling Green State University
1000 Fine Arts Center
Bowling Green, OH 43433
www.bgsu.edu

Brigham Young University
College of Fine Arts and Communication
Provo, UT 84602-6402
www.byu.edu

Brooks College Long Beach
Animation Multimedia
4825 E. Pacific Coast Hwy.
Long Beach, CA 90804
www.brookscollege.edu

California Institute of the Arts
24700 McBean Pkwy.
Valencia, CA 91355-2399
www.calarts.edu

Cartoon Animation Institute
3440 W. 8th St.
Los Angeles, CA 90005
www.cartoonmation.com

Centre for Arts and Technology
415 King St.
Fredericton, NB E3B 1E5
www.digitalartschool.com

Chapman University
Dodge College of Film and Media Arts
1 University Dr.
Orange, CA 92466
www.chapman.edu

Cogswell Polytechnical College
1175 Bordeaux Dr.
Sunnyvale, CA 94089
www.cogswell.edu

College of Business and Technology
8991 SW 107 Ave., Ste. 200
Miami, FL 33176
www.cbt.edu

College for Creative Studies
201 Kirey St.
Detroit, MI 48702
www.ccscad.edu

Columbia College
Film and Video Dept.
600 S. Michigan Ave.
Chicago, IL 60605
www.colum.edu

De Anza College
21250 Stevens Creek Blvd.
Cupertino, CA 95014
www.deanza.edu

Digital Evolutions–Smoky Hill High School
16100 E. Smoky Hill Rd.
Aurora, CO 80015
www.digital-evolutions.org

Digital Film Academy
630 Ninth Ave., Ste. 901
New York, NY 10036
www.digitalfilmacademy.com

Digital Media Arts College
3785 N. Federal Hwy.
Boca Raton, FL 35434
www.dmac-edu.org

DuBois Business College
1 Beaver Dr.
DuBois, PA 15801
www.dbcollege.com

Earthlight Pictures Animation Training
1332 Kenwood Rd.
Santa Barbara, CA 93109
www.earthlightpictures.com

East Los Angeles College
1301 Avenida Cesar Chavez
Monterey Park, CA 91754-6099
www.elac.edu

East Orange Campus High School
344 Prospect Ave.
East Orange, NJ 07017
www.campusanimation.com

Edinboro University of Pennsylvania
215 Meadville St.
Edinboro, PA 16444
www.edinboro.edu

Ex'pression College for Digital Arts
5601 Shellmound St.
Emeryville, CA 94608
www.expression.edu

Florida Atlantic University
Center for Electronic Communication
111 Las Olas Blvd.
Fort Lauderdale, FL 33301
www.animasters.com

Future Media Concepts–Miami
6303 Blue Lagoon Dr.
Miami, FL 33126
www.fmctraining.com

Grand Valley State University
School of Communication
1 Campus Dr.
Allendale, MI 49401
www.gvsu.edu

Grant MacEwan College
Visual Communication Design
10700-104 Ave.
Edmonton, AB T5P 2P7
www.macewan.ca

Harvard University
Carpenter Center for the Arts
24 Quincy St.
Cambridge, MA 02139
www.ves.fas.harvard.edu

International Academy of Design and Technology
39 John St.
Toronto, ON M5V 3G6
www.iadt.ca

Joe Kubert School of Cartoon and Graphic Art, Inc.
37 Myrtle Ave.
Dover, NJ 07801
www.kubertsworld.com

The Kansas City Art Institute
School of Design
4415 Warwick Rd.
Kansas City, MO 64111
www.kcai.edu

Long Island University–Brooklyn
Media Arts
University Pl.
Brooklyn, NY 11201
www.brooklyn.liu.edu

Loyola Marymount University
School of Film and Television
One LMU Dr., ME8240
Los Angeles, CA 90045-8347
www.lmu.edu

Memphis College of Art
Overton Park
1930 Poplar
Memphis, TN 88104-2764
www.mca.edu

Minneapolis College of Art and Design
2501 Stevens Ave. South
Minneapolis, MN 55404
www.mcad.edu

Mount Ida College
School of Design
777 Dedham St.
Newton, MA 02459
www.mountida.edu

New York University
School of Continuing and Professional Studies
121 Broadway, 8th Fl.
New York, NY 10003
www.scps.nyu.edu/departments/index.jsp

Northeastern University
Dept. of Visual Arts
222 Ryder Hall
Boston, MA 02115
www.animation.neu.edu

Ohio State University/ACCAD
Advanced Center for the Arts/Design
122 Kinnear Rd.
Columbus, OH 43212-116
http://accad.osu.edu

Parsons School of Design
66 Fifth Ave.
New York, NY 10011
www.parsons.edu

Platt (Media Arts) College–San Diego
6250 El Cajon Blvd.
San Diego, CA 92115-3919
www.platt.edu

Red River Community College
Digital Arts Dept.
400-123 Main St.
Winnipeg, MB R3C 1A3
www.rrc.mb.ca

Rhode Island School of Design
Film-Animation
2 College Rd.
Providence, RI 02905-6200
www.risd.edu

Rochester Institute of Technology
College of Imaging Arts and Sciences
1 Lomb Memorial Dr.
Rochester, NY 14623
www.rit.edu

Rocky Mountain College of Art and Design
6275 E. Evans Ave.
Denver, CO 20224
www.rmcad.edu

San Jose State University
School of Art and Design
1 Washington Square
San Jose, CA 95192
http://ad.sjsu.edu/home.html

Savannah College of Art and Design
P.O. Box 2072
Savannah, GA 32402-2042
www.scad.edu

School of the Art Institute of Chicago
37 S. Wabash Ave.
Chicago, IL 60603
www.saic.edu

School of the Visual Arts
209 E. 23rd St.
New York, NY 10010
www.schoolofvisualarts.edu

Springfield College
263 Alden St.
Springfield, MA 01119
www.spfldcol.edu

UCLA Animation Workshop
P.O. Box 951622
Los Angeles, CA 90095-1622
http://animation.filmtv.ucla.edu

University of Advancing Technology
2625 Baseline Rd.
Tempe, AZ 85283
www.uat.edu

University of the Arts
Media Arts Dept.
320 S. Broad St.
Philadelphia, PA 19102
www.uarts.edu

University of Colorado at Denver
Digital Animation Center
Campus Box 177, Box 173364
Denver, CO 80217-3364
www.cudenver.edu

University of Massachusetts Amherst
Arts Dept. and Fine Arts Ctr.
151 Presidents Dr.
Amherst, MA 01003
www.umass.edu

University of Southern California
School of Cinematic Arts
850 W. 35th St.
usc.edu

University of Texas–Dallas
Institute for Interactive Arts and Engineering
P.O. Box 830688
Richardson, TX 75083-0688
http://iiae.utdallas.edu

University of Utah
Arts Technology Program, College of Fine Arts
201 President's Circle, Rm. 201
Salt Lake City, UT 84112
www.artstech.utah.edu

University of Washington
Center for Digital Arts and Experimental Media
Box 353414
University of Washington
Seattle, WA 98195
www.washington.edu

VanArts, Vancouver Institute of Media Arts
837 Beatty St.
Vancouver, BC V6B 2M6
www.vanarts.com

Vancouver Film School
200-198 W. Hastings St.
Vancouver, BC V6B 1H2
www.vfs.com

Virtual Partners Training
1920 Libal St., Ste. 10A
Green Bay, WI 54301
www.virtualpartners.com

Winston-Salem State University
Fine Arts Dept.
601 Martin Luther King Jr. Dr.
Winston-Salem, NC 27110
www.wssu.edu

FURTHER READING

Newspaper and Magazine Articles

Astor, Dave. "The Growing Art of Cartoon Blogging." *Editor & Publisher*, June 1, 2006.

Bross, Tom. "Where Popeye and Hopalong Rule." *The Boston Globe*, May 2, 2004.

Brozan, Nadine. "Tall Dose of Respect for Comics." *Houston Chronicle*, August 14, 2005.

Corder, Katie. "Comic Pages Make Me Smile." *Spokane Spokesman Review*, June 14, 2004.

Dempsey, John. "Toons Got the Bugs Out." *Variety*, July 26, 2004.

Gusnue, John. "Drawing Conclusions." *St. John's Newfoundland Telegram*, March 24, 2005.

Sweet, Doug. "It's Time to Change the Comics." *Montreal Gazette*, January 1, 2004.

Vigil, Delfin. "Toon Town." *San Francisco Chronicle*, January 1, 2005.

Books on Cartooning

Blitz, Bruce. *The Big Book of Cartooning*. Running Press Book Publishers, 2006.

Clarkson, Mark. *Flash 5 Cartooning*. Muze, 2006.

Eisner, Will. *Comics and Sequential Art*. Poorhouse Press, 2001.

Hart, Christopher. *How to Draw Cartoons for Comic Strips*. Watson-Guptill Publications, 2003.

Hedge, Michael H. *Successful Syndication: A Guide for Writers and Cartoonists*, Allworth Press, 2000.

Hurd, Jud. *Cartoon Success Secrets*. Andrews and McMeel, 2004.

McCloud, Scott. *Making Comics*. Kitchen Sink Press, 2006.

Oliphant, Pat. *Oliphant's Presidents: Twenty-Five Years of Caricatures*. Andrews and McMeel, 2001.

Peters, Mike. *The World of Cartooning*. Landfall Press, 2005.

Robinson, Jerry. *The Comics: An Illustrated History of Comic Strip Art*. Dark Horse Comics, 2006.

Writer's Digest Books. *Artist's and Graphic Designer's Market*. Writer's Digest Books, 2006.

Writer's Digest Books. *Writer's Market*. Writer's Digest Books (annual).

Books on Animation

Amidi, Amid. *Cartoon Modern: Style and Design in 1950s Animation*. Chronicle Books, 2006.

Brasch, Walter. *Cartoon Monikers: An Insight into the Animation Industry*. Bowling Green University Press, 2003.

Brooks, Charles. *Best Editorial Cartoons of 2005*. Pelican Publishing, 2006.

Cagle, Daryl. *Best Political Cartoons of 2005*. Macmillan Computer Publishers, 2006.

The Funny Times Editors. *The Best of the Best American Humor*. Random House, 2002.

Hall, Ed, and Charles Brooks. *Diversions*. Halltoons, 2006.

Hanna, William and Joseph Barbera. *Art of Hanna and Barbera: Fifty Years of Creativity*. Hanna and Barbera, 2001.

King, Joe. *Funny Papers #4*. Trafford Publishing, 2004.

King, Joe. *Rust and Wrinkles*. Trafford Publishing, 2002.

Kirkpatrick, Glenn and Kevin Peaty. *Flash Cartoon Animation: Learn from the Pros*. Friends of Ed., 2002.

Palmer, Kate Salley. *Growing Up Cartoonist in the Baby Books*. Clemson Digital Press, 2006.

Rose, John. *Now This Is Where I Draw the Line*. Scripps Howard News Service, 2003.

Schulz, Charles M. *Charlie Brown*, 40th Anniversary Edition. Harper Paperbacks, 2005.

Sorensen, Jen. *Slowpoke American Gone Bonkers*. Macmillan Computer Publishing, 2005.

Watts, Paul. *Animation: Genre and Authorship*. Wallflower Press, 2002.

Williams, Richard. *The Animation Survival Kit: A Manual of Methods, Principles, and Format*. Faber and Faber, 2002.

Writer's Digest Books. *Writer's Market*, Writer's Digest Books (annual).

About the Author

Terence J. Sacks is an independent writer with more than thirty years of experience in communications. He has written dozens of news articles, magazine articles, and speeches as well as books. Sacks's articles have appeared in such publications as *LifeTimes*, *Hospitals*, *Chicago Medicine*, and *The Lion Magazine*. He has written books for McGraw-Hill, including *Careers in Medicine*, *Careers in Nursing*, *Opportunities in Funeral Service Careers*, *Opportunities in Physician Assistant Careers*, *Opportunities in Osteopathic Medicine Careers*, and *Opportunities in Cartooning and Animation Careers*.

A graduate of Northwestern's Medill School of Journalism, Sacks has written on many topics, but his credentials in health and medical topics are especially strong. From 1970 to 1973 he was director of communications for the Chicago Medical Society, the local group for physicians in Chicago and Cook County. He has also held positions in communications for the American Osteopathic Association, the American Association of Dental Schools, and several hospitals in Chicago.

For the past twenty years, Sacks has headed his own writing and communications firm, Terence J. Sacks Associates. He is active in the Independent Writers of Chicago (where he has served on the board), the American Medical Writers Association, and the Publicity Club of Chicago.